AUDEN AND CHRISTIANITY

Auden and Christianity

ARTHUR KIRSCH

Yale University Press   *New Haven & London*

Designed by James J. Johnson and set in New Caledonia Roman type
by Integrated Publishing Solutions.

Printed in the United States of America by Sheridan Books.

Library of Congress Cataloging-in-Publication Data

Kirsch, Arthur C.
Auden and Christianity / Arthur Kirsch.
p.   cm.
Includes bibliographical references (p.   ) and index.
ISBN 0-300-10814-1 (alk. paper)

1. Auden, W. H. (Wystan Hugh), 1907–1973. 2. Christian Biography—
England. 3. Poets, English—20th century—Biography.   I. Title.
BR1725.A86K57   2005
811′.52—dc22
2005003957

A catalogue record for this book is available from the British Library.

The paper in this book meets the guidelines for permanence and durability
of the Committee on Production Guidelines for Book Longevity
of the Council on Library Resources.

10 9 8 7 6 5 4 3 2 1

To Beverly,
and Matthew and Alice
and their families

CONTENTS

ACKNOWLEDGMENTS

I am greatly indebted to Edward Mendelson, whose works *Early Auden* and *Later Auden*, as well as his editions and bibliographies of Auden, have made Auden accessible and understandable to a generation of readers. This book would not have been possible without the foundation provided by his scholarship and by his generous personal help when I was editing Auden's *Lectures on Shakespeare* and *The Sea and the Mirror.* I also owe much to John Fuller's invaluable reader's guide to Auden's poetry, *W. H. Auden: A Commentary.* In addition, I have been helped by books and articles on Auden by many writers, including Geoffrey Grigson, Clive James, and Oliver Sacks. I owe a special debt to Ursula Niebuhr's rich and penetrating reminiscences of Auden, and to numerous conversations with a Congregationalist minister, Janet Legro, who read the entire manuscript of this book and contributed vital ideas drawn from her own experience and knowledge of Christianity.

I had generous assistance from Stephen Crook and Philip Milito at the Berg Collection of the New York Public Library. I am very grateful as well for the dedicated help of my editor at Yale University Press, John Kulka, as well as that of his editorial assistant, Mary Traester, and the manuscript editor, Lawrence Kenney.

I owe most, as usual, to the editorial experience, unfailing good judgment, and loving support of my wife, Beverly.

INTRODUCTION

In a review written in 1941, W. H. Auden chided the "prudery" of "cultured people, to whom . . . theological terms were far more shocking than any of the four-letter words," "whose childish memories associate religion with vague and pious verbiage." Such "prudery" has only intensified in recent decades, especially among academics and intellectuals who assume that one cannot be a religious and a thinking person at the same time. Auden stands as an eloquent example of the joining of the two, a modern instance of a person in whom thought and faith not only coexisted, but nourished each other. His faith expanded the horizons of his mind as well as his heart, and his formidable intelligence, in turn, probed the nature and limits of his Christian belief, animating his continuous quest not only to believe *still* but also to believe *again*.

Auden praised Saint Augustine for showing that "the Christian faith can make sense of man's private and social experience," and he explained his own faith in those terms. He wrote that as distinct from the presuppositions of "a faith which applies to some specialized activity," scientific research, for example, "there is the Faith by which a man lives his life as a man, i.e. the presuppositions he holds in order that 1. he may make sense of his past and present experience; 2. he may be able to act toward the future with a sense that his actions will be meaningful and effective; 3. that he and his world may be able to be changed from what they are into something more satisfactory. Such a faith can only be held dogmatically, for in man's historical and mortal existence, no experiment is ever identically repeatable." These presuppositions informed Auden's work as well as his life. In a talk at Columbia University in 1940, he remarked, "Art is not metaphysics . . . and the artist is usually unwise to insist too directly in his art upon his beliefs; but without an adequate and conscious metaphysics in the background, art's imitation of life inevitably becomes, either a photostatic copy of the accidental details of life without pattern or significance, or a personal allegory of the artist's individual dementia, of interest primarily to the psychologist and the historian." For Auden this integrating metaphysics was the Anglo-Catholic faith.

Auden's decision to write poetry was from the first associated with his faith. When he was fifteen years old, his friend Robert Medley attacked the Church while the two were walking together on a field near their school. Auden startled Medley by declaring that he was a believer. "An argument followed," Medley recalled, "and to soften what I feared might become a serious breach, after a pause, I asked him if he wrote poetry, confessing by way of exchange, that I did. I was a little surprised that he had not tried and suggested he might do so." Years later, Auden recollected the episode in "Letter to Lord Byron":

> Kicking a little stone, he turned to me
> And said, "Tell me, do you write poetry?"
> I never had, and said so, but I knew
> That very moment what I wished to do.

Auden "discovered" that he had "lost his faith" shortly after this conversation with Medley in 1922, and the association of a quarrel about religion with his decision to write poetry may have been accidental, but the collocation is suggestive, and one may note that Auden himself did not believe in random events.

In 1940 Auden formally returned to the liturgy and faith of his childhood, though his faith was never entirely absent in the intervening years, and thereafter Christianity is the governing subject of many of his most important long poems, including "For the Time Being: A Christmas Oratorio," *The Sea and the Mirror: A Commentary on Shakespeare's "The Tempest,"* and "Horae Canonicae," a series of poems corresponding to the church offices. Christianity is also part of the fabric of *The Double Man,* and it underlies such shorter poems, both before and after 1940, as "Musée des Beaux Arts" and "In Praise of Limestone," among a great many others. In 1939, in his unfinished prose work *The Prolific and the Devourer,* he began exploring the grounds of his faith in detail, and in 1942 he published anonymously a series of luminous essays on Christianity, including its relation to Judaism and anti-Semitism, in the Roman Catholic journal *The Commonweal.* In the remaining years of his life he wrote numerous essays and reviews dealing with religious subjects. He con-

stantly referred to, reviewed, or echoed such writers as Saint
Augustine, Pascal, Søren Kierkegaard, Martin Buber, Paul
Tillich, Reinhold Niebuhr, and Eugene Rosenstock-Huessy;
and his literary criticism in *The Enchafèd Flood* and *The Dyer's
Hand,* as well as in his yearlong series of lectures on Shakespeare at the New School for Social Research in New York, is
thoroughly informed by his faith. He testified to his own experience of a vision of agape both in his poem "A Summer
Night" in 1933 and in his introduction to Anne Fremantle's
The Protestant Mystics in 1964. Around 1947, he became active in a small ecumenical and distinguished religious discussion group in New York called The Third Hour as well as in
the larger Guild of Episcopal Scholars. Near the end of his
life he recapitulated the tenets of his belief in a comprehensive and eloquent essay on the intermingling of work, play,
and prayer in human life.

Auden's Christian faith can thus hardly be exaggerated,
but as a subject of study, it nonetheless poses difficulties.
Auden objected to analytical explanations of his own or anyone else's religious faith (he did so acerbically in the same
essay in which he explained the meaning of "the Faith by
which a man lives his life as a man"), and he did not welcome
most Christian apologetics. "Theology and 'Christian philosophy,'" he said, "are written by and for believers—persons, that
is, to whom God is already a subject of prayer, even if only sub-
consciously. Except in the context of prayer they are meaningless, for to talk *about* God, as one talks about the weather or
bimetallism, is to take His name in vain."

In addition, though Auden always stressed the human need
for the unconditional as a foundation of religious belief—he
called dogma "the right thinking which is to a way of life as its

grammar is to a language"—he also insisted, as he said in "New Year Letter," that "our faith" must be "well balanced by our doubt." "In a civilized society," he wrote in an essay in 1940, "that is, one in which a common faith is combined with a skepticism about its finality, and which agrees with Pascal that '*Nier, croire, et douter bien sont à l'homme ce que le courir est au cheval*' [to deny, to believe, and to doubt well are to man what the race is to the horse], orthodoxy can only be secured by a cooperation of which free controversy is an essential part." "Human law rests upon Force and Belief, belief in its rightness," Auden wrote in *The Prolific and the Devourer*, whereas "The Way rests upon Faith and Skepticism. Faith that the divine law exists, and that our knowledge of it can improve; and skepticism that our knowledge of these laws can ever be perfect: to have perfect knowledge we should have to know perfectly, i.e. become the universe." The relation of Auden's own doubts and beliefs was thus dialectical. His disposition to doubt extended to his conception of intelligence itself, whose "basic stimulus," he argued, "is doubt, a feeling that the meaning of an experience is not self-evident," but he remained acutely aware at the same time that skepticism, especially in matters of faith, must be founded upon reverence and that "to doubt for the sake of doubting, to differ for the sake of being different is pride."

Ursula Niebuhr, who, together with her husband, the eminent theologian Reinhold Niebuhr, was a good friend of Auden and welcomed him to her family, wrote in her tribute to him after his death that some academic theologians and clergymen who read him in the early 1940s, though pleased that a well-known poet would read theology, were also rather puzzled by his free use of theological categories. These "were supposed to be kept in their proper place, in their pigeon-holes, or indexed in their files, in the same way that clothes that they wore to church on Sunday were kept for their proper use. But Wystan was taking them out, and scattering the terms—and was wearing Sunday clothes on weekdays." "One of this ilk" asked her where Auden "stood" theologically. She was tempted, she said, "to tell my solemn interlocutor that Wystan never stood anywhere, only sat." Auden, however, took the question seriously when she told him about it afterward and gave her a characteristically open-minded answer: "Re my theological position, it is I think the same as your husband's, i.e. Augustinian not Thomist, (I would allow a little more place, perhaps, for the via negativa). Liturgically, I am Anglo Catholic, though not *too* spiky, I hope. As to forms of church organisation, I dont know what to think. I'm inclined to agree with de Rougemont that it will be back to the Catacombs for all of us. As to organisations, none of the churches look too hot, do they? But what organisation does?"

As Auden's statement suggests, Ursula Niebuhr's facetious reaction to her "solemn interlocutor" was appropriate. Though Auden was hardly averse to categories—he in fact loved them—his faith itself cannot be precisely categorized, and he would have distrusted anyone who presumed to do so. There are important recurring themes in his religious beliefs, but those beliefs are also not infrequently heterodox, marked by the controversies Auden said were indigenous to the Anglican Church, enacted in his work more than propounded, and so bound up with his temperament and his perception of his everyday life in the world, that to extract them into an abstract and systematic theology would be to falsify them. In a sermon he delivered in 1966 at Westminster Abbey, Auden said, "The Christian theologian is in the embarrassing position of having to use human language which by its nature is anthropomorphic to deny anthropomorphic conceptions of God." "Theological statements," he continued, "the Athanasian Creed for example, are neither poetic utterances nor logical propositions. They are—unfortunately theologians have not always recognized this—more like shaggy-dog stories— they have a point but if you try too hard to put your finger on it, you will miss it. St. Anselm was right—credo ut intelligam [I believe in order that I may understand]—but so was Tertullian—credo quia absurdum est [I believe because it is absurd]." Auden added that Tertullian's words were perhaps less shocking now than they were to the liberal humanists of the eighteenth and nineteenth centuries: "A few years ago, the physicist Wolfgang Pauli read a paper at a meeting of distinguished colleagues. During the discussion which followed, Niels Bohr got to his feet and said: 'We are all agreed that your theory is crazy. What divides us is whether it is crazy enough to stand a chance of being right. My own opinion is that it is not crazy enough.'"

In the same sermon Auden said, "Those of us who have the nerve to call ourselves Christians will do well to be extremely reticent on this subject. Indeed, it is almost the definition of a Christian that he is somebody who *knows* he isn't one, either in faith or morals." "Where faith is concerned," Auden continued, "very few of us have the right to say more than—to vary a saying of Simone Weil's—I believe in a God who is like the True God in everything except that he does not exist, for I have not yet reached the point where God exists." Directly after referring to Weil's remark in a series of notes on religion and theology he wrote in 1966–67, Auden commented, "The Church as a whole, seems to me loath to admit this. For instance, to build modern church buildings like an air-port . . . flooded with cheerful light, [is] a complete falsification of what we really feel; our hearts are not cheerful, and our heads are not clear." Auden wrote in "Friday's Child" in 1958 that we

> must put up with having learned
> All proofs or disproofs that we tender
> Of His existence are returned
> Unopened to the sender.

Though they have different emphases, neither this verse nor his reference to Simone Weil is a denial of faith. Both are assertions of his belief that man's fallen nature makes faith in God's existence a never-ending and difficult quest. In a letter to Clement Greenberg in 1944, he wrote, "A sinless life is like pure art. You must strive for it at the same time that you know it is impossible, and if you forget the impossibility, the life, like the poetry, ceases to be. (Incidentally, that's why I don't like Mondrian). Eternity is the decision *now*, the action now, one's neighbour *here*. And, as you know, for the Christian, the ultimate experience on this side of the resurrection is absolute failure and death. (My God, why hast thou forsaken me). The immortality of the soul is a Platonic, not a Christian doctrine."

A study of Auden's faith also runs the risk, sheerly by its focus, of creating an impression of religiosity that Auden would not have welcomed. He wrote that "of all the Christian Churches, not excluding the Roman Catholic, the Anglican Church has laid the most stress upon the institutional aspect of religion. Uniformity of rite has always seemed to her more important than uniformity of doctrine, and the private devo-

tions of her members have been left to their own discretion
without much instruction or encouragement from her." "Her
intellectual temper," he said, "is summed up in a remark by
one of her bishops, 'Orthodoxy is reticence.'" Auden believed
that "at its best," Anglican piety "shows spiritual good manners, a quality no less valuable in the religious life than in social life, though, of course, not the ultimate criterion in either,
reverence without religiosity, and humor (in which last trait it
resembles Jewish piety)." "Like all styles of piety," he said, "it
becomes detestable when the fire of love has gone out. It is no
insult to say that Anglicanism is the Christianity of a gentleman, but we know what a tiny hairbreadth there is between a
gentleman and a genteel snob." Auden suggests the same attitude, though less as a matter of manners, in discussing the
imbalance in Søren Kierkegaard's piety, his "overemphasis on
one aspect of the truth at the expense of all the others." He
strongly criticizes Kierkegaard's neglect of ordinary human
affections and quotes as correctives Dietrich Bonhoeffer's
declarations that "we ought not to try and be more religious
than God Himself," and that "we should love God eternally
with our whole hearts, yet not so as to compromise or diminish our earthly affections, but as a kind of cantus fermus to
which the other melodies of life provide the counterpoint."

Finally, I think Auden might have been wary of any academic study of his faith, however sympathetic or tactful, and
perhaps especially one written from the point of view of an
agnostic non-Christian. Auden was remarkably free of religious prejudice. He could, for example, tease Greenberg: "All
the same, Clem, I'm afraid you're really one of us—if for no
better reason than that you are a Jew, and the Jew is, willy-
nilly, 'chosen'"; and he could also describe the inclusiveness

of the Church in serious utopian terms. In a review written at the end of World War II, for example, he stated that the Christian "has to make his public confession of belief in a church which is not confined to his sort, to those with whom by nature he feels at home, for in it there is neither Jew nor German, East nor West, boy nor girl, smart nor dumb, boss nor worker, Bohemian nor bourgeois, no elite of any kind." "Indeed," Auden adds, in a sentence that anticipates his sermon at Westminster Abbey, "there are not even Christians there, for Christianity is a way, not a state, and a Christian is never something one is, only something one can pray to become." This passage, however, is immediately preceded by, and written in the context of, a discussion of Christian heresies in which Auden insists absolutely on the necessity of belief in the Incarnation, "the heroism of the Cross," Original Sin, and the forgiveness of sins: "If he is to become a Christian, a man has to believe them all." In one of his rare negative reviews, he expressed outrage at a book by Lewis Mumford that failed to acknowledge and explain its own amorphously skeptical assumptions and that treated Christian faith syncretically: "You can no more pick a treasury of the world's best doctrines and so make a faith you will believe in, than you can take a beautiful leg from one girl and a beautiful arm from another, and get a wife you will live with till you die. Hamlet cannot escape the trap of reflection by more reflecting."

I hope, in the study that follows, that I have been adequately conscious of such traps, and that I have not missed the point of Auden's own profound shaggy-dog stories. I quote often and at length from Auden's published prose and poetry, as well as from his draft notes, manuscripts, and letters, for which I ask the reader's patience, since I see this book as partly a work of description and appreciation, and as Auden himself remarked, such a work demands substantial quotations from the texts. Auden also suggested, in a letter to Monroe Spears, that his religion should be considered in the context of his writings. I have tried to abide by that advice, as the meaning of his Christian faith, to us as well as to him, cannot be understood apart from its incarnation in his work. Auden wrote, in *A Certain World,* "In this world, so long as we are vigorous enough to be capable of action, God, surely, does not intend us to sit around thinking of and loving Him like anything. Aside from rites of public worship in which we bring our bodies to God, we should direct our mental attention towards Him only for so long as it takes us to learn what He wills us to do here and now. This may take only a moment if the task he sets us is easy; if hard, a little longer. But once we know what it is, we should forget all about Him and concentrate our mental and physical energies upon our task." Auden's task, of course, was his art.

CHAPTER ONE

Early Years

Though generally reticent about his personal life, Auden wrote what he called a "rather shy-making" autobiographical essay about his Christian faith in 1956, observing that "the Christian doctrine of a personal God implies that the relation of every human being to Him is unique and historical, so that any individual who discusses the Faith is compelled to begin with autobiography." He pointed out that both of his grandfathers and four of his uncles were Anglican priests, and that the atmosphere of his home "was, I should say, unusually devout, though not in the least repressive or gloomy. My parents were Anglo-Catholics, so that my first religious memories are of exciting magical rites (at six I was a boat-boy) rather than of listening to sermons." "For this," he said, "I am very grateful, as it implanted in me what I believe to be the correct notion of worship, namely, that it is first and foremost a community in action, a thing done together, and

only secondarily a matter of individual feeling or thinking."
Auden always considered sermons extrinsic to worship and
avoided them whenever he could. In his draft notes on religion and theology he said, "In my opinion sermons should be
a) fewer b) longer c) more theologically instructive and less
exhortatory. I must confess that in my life I have very seldom
heard a sermon from which I derived any real spiritual ben-
efit. Most of them told me that I should love God and my
neighbour more than I do, but that I knew already." But the
rituals of worship forever interested him. Services on Sunday
when he was a boy included "music, candles and incense,"
and "at Christmas a crèche was rigged up in the dining-
room, lit by an electric-torch battery, round which we sang
hymns." Auden cherished such childhood memories, and his
association of the ceremoniousness and rituals of the liturgy
with the music and magical thinking of his childhood was an
irreducible element of his faith. He always assumed that the
liturgy is an action that can actually change people, as art
cannot.

Two other "saving" influences affected Auden when he was
a boy and a young man. First, he said, he was "lucky enough
to have a voice and a musical sense" that allowed him to be a
member of school choirs, first as a student and later as a
teacher, and that consequently, "however bored I might be at
the thought of God, I enjoyed services in His worship very
much, more, probably, than many who were more devout
than I but who had no active role to play." Second, he "was
lucky enough to be born in a period when every educated person was expected to know the Bible thoroughly" (all under-
graduates, for example, were required to pass a divinity exam-
ination) and that, consequently, "whatever attitude one might

take towards the Bible, that it was great literature, an interesting anthropological document, or what have you, the events
and sayings upon which Christianity is founded were as familiar to one as Grimm's fairy tales."

The analogy between Christianity and Grimm's fairy tales
is revealing. Ursula Niebuhr noted that the imagery and mythology of theology fascinated Auden, feeding his imagination
and making him "much more theological than many academic
theologians." The poetic fascination with the language and images as well as the rites of Christian worship—again associated
with memories of childhood—lasted Auden's entire lifetime
and helps account for his outraged response to the reform of
the liturgy in his later years, especially to the reading of "the
Epistle and Gospel . . . in some appalling 'modern' translation." As opposed to Roman Catholics, he said, who had to
start from scratch with their vernacular liturgy, "we had the extraordinary good fortune in that our Book of Common Prayer
was composed at exactly the right historical moment. The English language had become more or less what it is today," and
"the ecclesiastics of the sixteenth century still possessed a feeling for the ritual and ceremoniousness which today we have almost entirely lost. Why should we spit on our luck?"

Auden was also drawn to the communal service of the
liturgy because of his lifelong sense of isolation. As his many
friends testified, Auden had a wish, and a gift, for friendship;
he was intellectually exuberant and good-hearted; and he was
fun to be with. At the same time, however, his warmth was accompanied, as a university friend remarked, by "the sharp-
ness and power of his ice-cold imagination." Other friends,
early and late, wrote of his essential shyness and loneliness,
and in numerous essays Auden himself spoke of the difficulty

he had in fully believing in and accepting the existence of other people. "At sometime or other in human history," he wrote in 1932, "when and how is not known exactly, man became self-conscious; he began to feel, I am I, and You are Not-I; we are shut inside ourselves and apart from each other. There is no whole but the self." "The more this feeling grew," Auden continued, the more man "felt the need to bridge over the gulf, to recover the sense of being as much part of life as the cells in his body are part of him."

These statements reveal a preoccupation that was to absorb Auden for the rest of his life. In this early essay, he argued that human speech evolved to bridge the gulf, and in later essays he treated it more as a religious issue, quoting Simone Weil's statement, for example, that "belief in the existence of other human beings as such is love." But his own basic sense of apartness remained a fulcrum of his thinking and temperament. This was to some degree a result of a clinical disposition he had inherited from his father, who was a physician. Christopher Isherwood remarked in 1937 that Auden had acquired a "scientific outlook and technique of approach" and was particularly fond of the word *clinical*. Stephen Spender—never free of envy of Auden's talent and fame—said, less charitably, of Auden's clinical inclinations that "Auden, despite his perceptiveness, lacked something in human relationships. He forced issues too much, made everyone too conscious of himself and therefore was in the position of an observer who is a disturbing force in the behaviour he observes. Sometimes he gave the impression of playing an intellectual game with himself and with others, and this meant that in the long run he was rather isolated." Spender doubted if Auden "completely broke away from the isolation in human relationships which was simply the result of his overwhelming cleverness as a very young man." Auden himself wrote to Spender in 1940, "As you know my dominant faculties are intellect and intuition, my weak ones feeling and sensation. This means I have to approach life via the former; I must have knowledge and a great deal of it before I can feel anything"; and he wrote in an article in the same year that he was attracted to Thomas Hardy's poetry when he was young "because I half suspected that my own nature was both colder and more mercurial, and I envied those who found it easy to feel deeply."

Auden was also isolated by his homosexuality, the practice of which was a criminal offense in both Britain and the United States for most of his lifetime. His boyhood friend Robert Medley said that "Wystan was and felt himself to be alone; set apart by the crucial experience of the self-realization that he had to face up to, and in which he had refused to deny his nature and the source of his creative being." Writing of his later years, his brother John said, "In spite of his fame and wide friendships throughout America and Europe, he was lonely, lacking as a result of his personal psychology, a family of his own, but remembering our own happy early years. . . . Seen unawares in an armchair, *The Times* crossword puzzle on his knee, a vodka martini by his side and cigarette-ends covering large dishes, there was an isolation and sadness which arose from his uprooted and solitary existence." Auden himself said in a commencement address at Smith College that "each of us" must accept "the fact that in the last analysis we live our lives alone. Alone we choose, alone we are responsible. So many people try to forget their aloneness, and break their heads and hearts against it." Auden also often referred to Kierkegaard's religious sense of "always being out alone over seventy thousand fathoms," and in "New Year Letter" he wrote, "Aloneness is man's real condition." Toward the end of his life, Auden directly related his faith to his sense of isolation, writing in a notebook, "In every man there is a loneliness, an inner chamber of peculiar life into which God only can enter." One may speculate that for such a temperament the worship of the liturgy, "first and foremost a community in action, a thing done together, and only secondarily a matter of individual feeling or thinking," would have satisfied a deep need, providing not only continuity with his past but also a communal sanctuary, a refuge from the isolating tendencies of his intellect, his personality, and his situation. Auden said he was sorry that his deeply religious friend Dag Hammerskjöld, the secretary general of the United Nations, had not participated "in the liturgical and sacramental life of a church. . . . because it is precisely the introverted intellectual character who stands most in need of the ecclesiastical routine both as a discipline and as a refreshment." *"In solitude, for company,"* Auden wrote in the refrain of "Lauds," the poem in "Horae Canonicae" that celebrates worship.

In early adolescence, Auden lapsed from his childhood belief. "At thirteen," he wrote, "I was confirmed. To say that shortly afterwards I lost my faith would be melodramatic and false. I simply lost interest." The time of lost interest was the period in the 1920s and 1930s in which his work was more apparently preoccupied with politics and psychology and in which he eventually became celebrated as an artistic spokesman for his generation. Auden attributed the lapse in his interest in religion to several factors. As a young man, he said, he had a natural wish to assert his independence and "enjoy the pleasures of the world and the flesh," and he also became disenchanted with the motives of apparently religious people around him. He observed that many Christians were merely conventionally Christian, believing the Nicene Creed as they believed in proper manners or proper dress, and that many others were consciously unbelievers, Christian only officially, in order to fulfill a condition of their employment. He also felt that the religiousness of many ardent believers seemed to be prompted by some mental or physical infirmity. Behind his own youthful *Schwärmerai*, he said, his "pseudo-devout phase" of religious enthusiasm, for example, "lay a quite straightforward and unredeemed eroticism." He was therefore "apt . . . to draw the conclusion that people only love God when no one else will love them." Finally, he remarked, he became acutely conscious of "the gulf between the language and imagery of [the Church's] liturgies and devotions and those of contemporary culture. . . . *Agnus Dei* has the attraction, at least, of a magical and musical spell; *Lamb of God,* in a culture, mainly urban, to which the notion of animal sacrifice is totally strange, is liable to evoke ridiculous images." Thus, having just reached an age when personal belief became "possible," he found that "the terms in which the Church" expected "him to think about God (as distinct, of course, from *what* she expects him to think)" were not terms in which either he or any of his contemporaries, "Christian or not," could "think, sincerely or accurately, of anything."

In a sense, Auden never entirely abandoned such reservations, even after his return to the Church in 1940, and they were always a stimulus to his faith, to what he considered the process of becoming, rather than simply being, a Christian. Late in his life he wrote, "Every Christian has to make the transition from the child's 'We believe still' to the adult's 'I believe again.' This cannot have been easy to make at any time, and in our age it is rarely made, it would seem, without a hiatus of unbelief." Auden tended to see the continuing enactment of this transition in adult life as peculiarly Protestant. In a review of Reinhold Niebuhr's *The Nature and Destiny of Man* in 1941 he wrote that "the Catholic emphasizes the initial act of intellectual assent" in his faith, "the Protestant the continuous process of voluntary assent." He added, "The former is therefore always in danger of identifying the eternal with some particular historical social form; the latter is always in danger of ignoring the concrete realities of a historical situation altogether"; and he praised Niebuhr's "balanced statement of orthodox Protestantism" for its clear consciousness of those realities. Decades later, making essentially the same distinction about belief, he said that in his relation to God, "it is personal experience which enables me to add to the catholic *We believe still* the protestant *I believe again.*" He also wrote in a notebook, however, without any sectarian emphasis, that the "liturgy uses *we* for the general confession, because each of us is in part responsible for the sins of our neighbour, but in the creed it says *credo,* not *credamus*—nobody can put the responsibility for his faith upon others." He noted that in the rite of Baptism "promises are made on behalf of the child by its godparents," whereas in the rite of Confirmation the confirmand is fully aware of what he is saying and "gives his personal assent to a life-long commitment to the faith." Confirmation should thus "be postponed until the individual has reached the age of spiritual consent, which in the average case can well be over 25. Child confirmation is as absurd as child marriage."

Auden exaggerated his faithlessness as a young man, since many of his interests in that period were really an attempt to find an alternate, though still Christian, epistemology. He said as much himself: "The various 'kerygmas,' of Blake, of Lawrence, of Freud, of Marx, to which, along with most middle-class intellectuals of my generation, I paid attention between twenty and thirty, had one thing in common." "They were all," he noted, "Christian heresies; that is to say, one cannot imagine their coming into existence except in a civilization which claimed to be based, religiously, on belief that the Word was made flesh and dwelt among us, and that, in consequence, matter, the natural order, is real and redeemable, not a shadowy appearance or the cause of evil, and historical time is real and significant, not meaningless or an endless series of cycles." These are distinctions that animated Auden's thought and work throughout his career.

The Orators: An English Study, a long, hectic, brilliant, and often obscure work in a mixture of verse and prose that Auden published in 1932, offers some evidence of such a Christian background. There are biblical allusions throughout the poem, and it seems haunted by a remembered faith, especially in the opening sections. In "Address for a Prize-Day," Auden refers admiringly to *The Divine Comedy* and uses Dante's division of sinners into three main groups in the *Purgatorio* to describe contemporary "England, this country of ours where nobody is well." Auden's citations of Dante are not entirely accurate, and the tone of the address has a manic and satiric edge, but the aura of the *Purgatorio* is nonetheless present. A subsequent section has transparent Christian overtones in Auden's parodic description of an anxious search for an absent Leader. The final sentence of the section, "The priest's mouth opens in the green graveyard, but the wind is against it," maintains the parodic tone, but the reference to the priest is elegiac as well.

Other early poems and references also show Auden's Christian preoccupations. His juvenile poem "Narcissus" begins with an epigraph from the *Confessions* of Saint Augustine; and in a letter to William McAlwee on Good Friday 1928 mentioning that he was still revising the poem, he wrote, partly but not entirely jokingly, "Jesus died to-day." In 1929, in the first section of "It was Easter as I walked in the public gardens," Auden remembers the death that precedes Easter's regeneration and looks back to "Christmas intimacy." The sense of renewal of the Resurrection is evoked as well in the conclusion of the poem. The poem also explores, among other themes, one's psychological need to break away from one's parents, and, as Auden wrote in his 1929 journal, that involves "liberation from the superego, obeyed like the parents whom Christ enjoined us to abandon." He noted, in the same journal, that "the point of psychology is to prove the Gospel." A correspondent asked him about Freud's influence on another early poem, "O what is that sound which so thrills the ear?" and Auden answered, "Freud if you like. The idea came from a picture I saw of the Agony in the Garden, with the soldiers in the distance."

But Auden's Christian promptings were also explicit in this early period. In 1933, in "A Summer Night," during a phase of his life when he was especially preoccupied with the divisions between public and private worlds and with his own sense of isolation, he celebrated a mystical experience of community with several colleagues at Downs School, where he was teaching. He wrote, in the early stanzas of the poem,

Equal with colleagues in a ring
I sit on each calm evening
   Enchanted as the flowers
The opening light draws out of hiding
With all its gradual dove-like pleading,
   Its logic and its powers.

That later we, though parted then,
May still recall these evenings when
   Fear gave his watch no look;
The lion griefs loped from the shade
And on our knees their muzzles laid,
   And Death put down his book.

Now north and south and east and west
Those I love lie down to rest;
   The moon looks on them all,
The healers and the brilliant talkers,
The eccentrics and the silent walkers,
   The dumpy and the tall.

The kind of experience Auden describes need not be specifically Christian, or perhaps even religious, but for Auden it
was. Worshippers formed a psychic field of a ring after the
feast of agape, the religious meal of the Lord's Supper, which
was associated with (though also differentiated from) the Eucharist in the early Christian Church, and a ring or circle always had sacramental and paradisal associations for him. In
later years, in the poem "In Sickness and in Health," Auden
celebrated the "round O of faithfulness we swear" represented by the wedding ring, and in *The Sea and the Mirror*, in
her imagination of paradise, Miranda, "remembering our
changing garden," speaks of being "linked as children in a
circle dancing." The "dove-like" light and the Edenic absence

of griefs and death both suggest a Christian experience, and
the sense of universal inclusiveness—the healers and talkers,
eccentrics and walkers, the dumpy and the tall—parallels
Auden's later understanding of the community in which "we
are all members one of another, mutually dependent and mutually responsible." The same understanding of the human
community underlies his memorable description of the
drunk in his essay on Shakespeare's *Henry IV:* "The drunk is
unlovely to look at, intolerable to listen to, and his self-pity is
contemptible. Nevertheless, as not merely a worldly failure
but also a willful failure, he is a disturbing image for the sober
citizen. His refusal to accept the realities of this world, baby-
ish as it may be, compels us to take another look at this world
and reflect upon our motives for accepting it." "The drunk-
ard's suffering," Auden continues, "may be self-inflicted, but
it is real suffering and reminds us of all the suffering in this
world which we prefer not to think about because, from the
moment we accepted this world, we acquired our share of responsibility for everything that happens in it."

In his introduction to Anne Fremantle's *The Protestant
Mystics* in 1964, three decades after writing "A Summer
Night," Auden returned to the experience represented in the
poem and described it explicitly as an example of "a vision of
agape." He attributed the description of the vision to someone whom he does not identify, but there can be little doubt
that it is his own:

> One fine summer night in June 1933 I was sitting on a
> lawn after dinner with three colleagues, two women and
> one man. We liked each other well enough but we were
> certainly not intimate friends, nor had any one of us a sex-

ual interest in another. Incidentally, we had not drunk any alcohol. We were talking casually about everyday matters when, quite suddenly and unexpectedly, something happened. I felt myself invaded by a power which, though I consented to it, was irresistible and certainly not mine. For the first time in my life I knew exactly—because, thanks to the power, I was doing it—what it means to love one's neighbor as oneself. I was also certain, though the conversation continued to be perfectly ordinary, that my three colleagues were having the same experience. (In the case of one of them, I was able later to confirm this.) My personal feelings towards them were unchanged—they were still colleagues, not intimate friends—but I felt their existence as themselves to be of infinite value and rejoiced in it.

I recalled with shame the many occasions on which I had been spiteful, snobbish, selfish, but the immediate joy was greater than the shame, for I knew that, so long as I was possessed by this spirit, it would be literally impossible for me deliberately to injure another human being. I also knew that the power would, of course, be withdrawn sooner or later and that, when it did, my greeds and self-regard would return. The experience lasted at its full intensity for about two hours when we said good-night to each other and went to bed. When I awoke the next morning, it was still present, though weaker, and it did not vanish completely for two days or so. The memory of the experience has not prevented me from making use of others, grossly and often, but it has made it much more difficult for me to deceive myself about what I am up to when I do. And among the various factors which several years later brought me back to the Christian faith in which I had been brought up, the memory of this experience and asking myself what it could mean was one of the most crucial, though, at the time it occurred, I thought I had done with Christianity for good.

Auden had not then done with Christianity for good, of course, as the 1933 poem alone shows, and the poem describes an experience whose memory Auden continuously sought to regain. The idea of agape is synonymous with the term *caritas* in Scripture, as well as with the love-feast of the early Church, and both senses of the word are evident in the poem as well as in the later prose account of the experience.

At around the same time he wrote "A Summer Night," Auden also wrote a review praising Violet Clifton's biography of her husband, *The Book of Talbot.* Quoting Henry James's remark, "Yes, the circumstances of the interest are there, but where is the interest itself?," Auden said he found the interest itself of *The Book of Talbot* in the completeness of Clifton's love of her husband. Her book showed, he said, that "the first criterion of success in any human activity, the necessary preliminary, whether to scientific discovery or to artistic vision, is intensity of attention or, less pompously, love. Love has allowed Lady Clifton to constellate round Talbot the whole of her experience and to make it significant." In a poem written a year earlier, Auden directly united James's remark with the idea of the ring of agape, locating "Love, the interest itself" in the human heart, "in the ring where name and image meet."

By the later 1930s, Auden's interest in Christianity became increasingly stronger and explicit. Isherwood remarked in 1937, after collaborating with Auden on several works, that Auden "enjoyed a high Anglican upbringing, coupled with a sound musical education. The Anglicanism has evaporated, leaving only the height: he is still much preoccupied with ritual, in all its forms. When we collaborate, I have to keep a sharp eye on him—or down flop the characters on their knees

(see *F6 passim*): another constant danger is that of choral in-
terruptions by angel-voices. If Auden had his way, he would
turn every play into a cross between grand opera and high
mass." Isherwood's own atheism at the time is likely to have
caused him to underestimate Auden's underlying sensitivity
to the religious significance of ritual. The word "evaporated,"
in any case, is an exaggeration.

By 1938, issues of Christian faith become quite unmistakable in Auden's work. The ending of "As I walked out one
evening" (1938) is especially notable. The first half of this
well-known poem describes the hopes of romantic love, and
the second half describes the conquest of such love by Time.
But the poem concludes with an affirmation:

> "O look, look in the mirror,
>   O look in your distress;
> Life remains a blessing
>   Although you cannot bless.
>
> "O stand, stand at the window
>   As the tears scald and start;
> You shall love your crooked neighbour
>   With your crooked heart."
>
> It was late, late in the evening,
>   The lovers they were gone;
> The clocks had ceased their chiming,
>   And the deep river ran on.

All three of these stanzas assert religious beliefs that were
to become important to Auden. "Life remains a blessing" became a refrain of his existence. In a tribute to him after his
death, his close friend Hannah Arendt wrote in exasperation,
"Time and again, when to all appearances he could not cope

any more, when his slum apartment was so cold that the
water no longer functioned . . . when his suit . . . was covered
with spots or worn so thin that his trousers would suddenly
split from top to bottom, in brief, whenever disaster hit before your very eyes, he would begin to kind of intone an utterly idiosyncratic, absurdly eccentric version of 'count your
blessings.'" Counting his blessings, however, was more than
just Auden's idiosyncratic response to his circumstances, self-
created or otherwise. It also expressed his religious conviction that "happiness consists in a loving and trusting relation
to God" and that it is "our eternal duty to be happy," a duty to
which "all considerations of pleasure and pain are subordi-
nate. Thou shalt love God and thy neighbour and Thou shalt
be happy mean the same thing." In the essay "The Giving of
Thanks" in 1944, he said, "for the gift of being alive, Miranda's
simple *O Wonder!*" is the proper expression of gratitude.
"And for what we all know in our hearts to be a gift though we
must never think of it as such for others," he added, "the gift
of suffering, Dante's honest, *I say pain but ought to say sol-
ace,* will do." In his commencement address at Smith College, he remarked, "All freedom implies necessity, that is to
say, suffering. The only suffering that can be avoided is the
terror of running away from it. If you will forgive my saying
so, I think if America has a national vice it is thinking suffering vulgar and purely negative."

In the next stanza, the command "You shall love your
crooked neighbour / With your crooked heart," as Edward
Mendelson observes, "does not refute its biblical original, but
explains it." In addition to the assumption that loving one's
neighbor is a choice, not a necessity, and therefore must be
commanded, the lines also suggest Auden's realization of the

need to open his homosexuality to forgiveness. "Crooked-
ness" had a sexual connotation for him. Isherwood reported
that when Auden gave him a copy of Robert Bridges's *The
Testament of Beauty,* he inscribed it "with four lines of the
very purest Auden":

> He isn't like us
> He isn't a crook
> The man is a heter
> Who wrote this book.

Auden never wholly approved of his homosexuality, but he
nonetheless took comfort in the belief that he was God's creature, that God made the universe and saw that it was good,
and that if homosexuality was a sin, it was an instance of man's
sinful condition and could be forgiven. To love your crooked
neighbor with your crooked heart was thus, for him, an inter-
nalization of the biblical injunction, a religious understanding
and alleviation of his own sense of isolation and a movement
toward the self-forgiveness that was the necessary condition
for his love of his neighbor.

In the final stanza of "As I walked out one evening," the
cessation of the clocks draws the poem back from the world
of time, the world of lovers' vows depicted in the earlier stanzas. A few years later, Auden made the scriptural basis of his
thoughts on time mordantly explicit:

> What right have I to swear
> Even at one a. m.
> To love you till I die?
>
> Earth meets too many crimes
> For fibs to interest her;
> If I can give my word,

> Forgiveness can recur
> Any number of times
> In Time. Which is absurd.
>
> *Tempus fugit.* Quite.
> So finish up your drink.
> *All flesh is grass.* It is.

Isaiah 40. 6–8 reads, "All flesh is grass, and all the goodliness thereof is as the flower of the field. . . . but the word of our God shall stand for ever." "And the deep river ran on," the final line of "As I walked out one evening," hints at this timeless world and perhaps intimates as well that nature is unaffected by human sorrow.

Such a view of nature is powerfully represented in another poem Auden wrote in 1938, "Musée des Beaux Arts," which depicts "the human position" of suffering in the dispassionate landscape of the daily life of man as well as of nature:

> About suffering they were never wrong,
> The Old Masters: how well they understood
> Its human position; how it takes place
> While someone else is eating or opening a window or just
>   walking dully along;
> How, when the aged are reverently, passionately waiting
> For the miraculous birth, there always must be
> Children who did not specially want it to happen, skating
> On a pond at the edge of the wood:
> They never forgot
> That even the dreadful martyrdom must run its course
> Anyhow in a corner, some untidy spot
> Where the dogs go on with their doggy life and the
>   torturer's horse
> Scratches its innocent behind on a tree.

In the second stanza, Auden focuses on Brueghel's painting of the fall of Icarus, a figure often interpreted as a type of Christ, and describes

> how everything turns away
> Quite leisurely from the disaster; the ploughman may
> Have heard the splash, the forsaken cry,
> But for him it was not an important failure; the sun shone
> As it had to on the white legs disappearing into the green
> Water; and the expensive delicate ship that must have
>   seen
> Something amazing, a boy falling out of the sky,
> Had somewhere to get to and sailed calmly on.

This poem, one of Auden's masterpieces, and one of the greatest poems ever written on painting, shows Auden's intense interest in understanding Christian history in the context of ordinary existence. In the first stanza, the untroubled life of children, dogs, horses, as well as of the natural landscape, in the presence of the Nativity and the Crucifixion appears to evoke Brueghel's painting *The Numbering at Bethlehem,* which Auden would have seen in the Musée des Beaux Arts in Brussels. The painting depicts the Gospel story of Joseph and Mary in a copiously detailed contemporary Flemish landscape, making their way to the tax collector through a crowd of people including children playing and throwing snowballs and adults doing their everyday tasks: sweeping snow, building a cabin, slaughtering a pig. Possibly, Auden may also have been thinking of Brueghel's *Winter Landscape with Skaters and a Bird Trap,* a scene of children skating on a pond, as well as *The Slaughter of the Innocents,* a village scene in which a host of soldiers are calmly killing children, while dogs run and play, and horses stand imperturbably tethered to posts. Auden's second stanza describes Brueghel's *Land-scape with the Fall of Icarus*, also in the Musée des Beaux Arts, which shows a shepherd calmly leaning on his staff, accompanied by his dog and surrounded by his sheep, a plough-man at work, a fisherman tending his line, and a ship sailing unaware close by, while the legs of Icarus, small and almost unnoticeable, are disappearing into the sea, his body already submerged. Both stanzas of "Musée des Beaux Arts" derive their power from the juxtaposition of momentous suffering with the unconcerned lives of ordinary people. Auden was to develop such contrasts at length in "Horae Canonicae," a poem in which ordinary people can be equally unobservant and at the same time agents of the Crucifixion.

Auden had little interest in eschatology. "There may or not be a supernatural world," he wrote, "but to think like Pascal that its existence or non-existence should make any difference to our life here, is to suppose a suspension in the chain of causality, or rather a division into two streams, one operating normally in this world, and the other mysteriously arrested, to begin operating mysteriously after death." "This is the sin against the Holy Ghost, which is to deny the Unity of Truth." "The Divine Law," Auden insists, "whatever its nature, operates here and now. As Kafka says: 'Only our concept of Time makes it possible for us to speak of the Day of Judgement by that name; in reality it is a summary court in perpetual session.'" Though he believed in miracles—he classified his own life and individuality as a miracle—Auden also was to have continued doubts about whether the Resurrection "really happened," as he put it to Ursula Niebuhr. In "Friday's Child," a poem on the Crucifixion, he wrote, "Now, did He really break the seal / And rise again? We dare not say," and he was sympathetic to Weil's statement that "if the Gospels omitted all mention of Christ's resurrection, faith would be easier for me. The Cross by itself suffices me." In his draft notes on religion and theology, Auden wrote, "To-day, we find Good Friday easy to accept: what scandalises us is Easter: Modern man finds a happy ending, a final victory of Love over the Prince of this World, very hard to swallow." He said elsewhere that "despite appearances to the contrary, the Christian faith, by virtue of its doctrines about creation, the nature of man, and the revelation of Divine purpose in historical time, was really a more this-worldly religion than any of its competitors"; and he remarked that as opposed to Buddha, Mahomet, Confucius, "Jesus convinces me he was right because . . . he forecast our historical evolution correctly. If we reject the Gospels, then we must reject modern life." He said in a letter to Clement Greenberg that faith is the opposite of "a withdrawal from the world. (Jesus said My kingdom is not of *this* world. He did not say of *the* world)."

In 1939, the year following the composition of "As I walked out one evening" and "Musée des Beaux Arts," Auden emigrated to the United States. Not long after, he tentatively started attending services at St. Mark's in the Bouwerie, an Episcopal church near his home in New York, and he reaffirmed his faith in October 1940, though the process of conversion was gradual, and as Auden wrote in a letter to Monroe Spears, the precise date should not be overdramatized. Auden ascribed his return to the Anglican Communion to a number of causes. The first was the "novelty and shock of the Nazis," who "made no pretense of believing in justice and liberty for all, and attacked Christianity on the grounds that to love one's neighbor as oneself was a command fit only for effeminate weaklings, not for the 'healthy blood of the master race.'" "Unless one was prepared to take a relativist view that all values are a matter of personal taste," he said, "one could hardly avoid asking the question: 'If, as I am convinced, the Nazis are wrong and we are right, what is it that validates our values and invalidates theirs?'" Auden also spoke, in an interview in the *Observer*, of his experience in November 1939 in a movie theater in Yorkville, a largely German section of Manhattan, at the showing of *Sieg im Polen*, an account by the Nazis of their conquest of Poland. When Poles appeared on the screen, Auden said, a number of "quite ordinary, supposedly harmless Germans in the audience were shouting, 'Kill the Poles.'" "I wondered then why I reacted as I did against this denial of every humanistic value. The answer brought me back to the church."

A second source of his religious renewal, Auden said, was a visit to Barcelona in January 1937, during the Spanish Civil War, in which he found as he walked through the city "that all the churches were closed and there was not a priest to be seen. To my astonishment, this discovery left me profoundly shocked and disturbed. . . . I could not escape acknowledging that, however I had consciously ignored and rejected the Church for sixteen years, the existence of churches and what went on in them had all the time been very important to me. If that was the case, what then?" Both these events, the rise of the Nazis and the destruction of the churches in Spain, antedate Auden's formal conversion by several years, and his reactions to both suggest, as do his writings in the late thirties, that his faith was reviving. The two experiences also show, as his work habitually does, his deep spiritual responsiveness to the world outside him as well as to the one within him.

Auden mentioned in addition that shortly after his visit to Barcelona, he met "an Anglican layman, and for the first time in my life I felt myself in the presence of personal sanctity." The man was Charles Williams, whose works Auden came greatly to admire and whose history of the Christian Church, *The Descent of the Dove*, led him to "read some theological works, Kierkegaard in particular," and to begin "going, in a tentative and experimental sort of way, to church." Kierkegaard's belief that a man is related in his life to an unconditional absolute that he must continuously search for but never fully know, resonated profoundly with Auden's own spiritual instincts of faith and doubt, as did Kierkegaard's consequent exploration of man's existential relationship with God in his everyday life.

A final cause of his conversion, Auden said, was that he was providentially "forced to know in person what it is like to feel oneself the prey of demonic powers, in both the Greek and the Christian sense, stripped of self-control and self-respect, behaving like a ham actor in a Strindberg play." The demonic experience to which he refers was his response to the betrayal by his lover Chester Kallman. Auden had met Kallman, an American fourteen years his junior, in April 1939, after his emigration to the United States, had fallen in love, a love he had sought, he said, since he was a child, and had entered into a relationship with him that he regarded as the moral equivalent of a marriage. In July 1941 Kallman revealed that he had betrayed him with another lover. At some point afterward Auden apparently put his hands around Kallman's throat while he was sleeping, but Kallman simply brushed him away. On Christmas Day 1941, he wrote a passionate letter to Kallman that reveals the extraordinary extent to which erotic and religious imagery had become fused in his imagination:

> Because it is in you, a Jew, that I, a Gentile, inheriting an O-so-genteel anti-semitism, have found my happiness:
> As this morning I think of Bethlehem, I think of you.

. . . .

> Because, suffering on your account the torments of sexual jealousy, I have had a glimpse of the infinite vileness of masculine conceit;
> As this morning, I think of Joseph, I think of you.

. . . .

> Because, on account of you, I have been, in intention, and almost in act, a murderer;
> As this morning I think of Herod, I think of you.

. . . .

> Because I believe in your creative gift, and because I rely absolutely upon your critical judgement,
> As this morning I think of the Magi, I think of you.

> Because you alone know the full extent of my human weakness, and because I think I know yours, because of my resentment against being small and your resentment against having a spinal curvature, and because with my body I worship yours;
> As this morning I think of the Manhood, I think of you.

> Because it is through you that God has chosen to show me my beatitude,
> As this morning I think of the Godhead, I think of you.

> Because in the eyes of our bohemian friends our relationship is absurd;
> As this morning I think of the Paradox of the Incarnation, I think of you.

Because, although our love, beginning Hans Andersen, became Grimm, and there are probably even grimmer tests
to come, nevertheless I believe that if only we have faith in
God and in each other, we shall be permitted to realize all
that love is intended to be;

> As this morning I think of the Good Friday and the
> Easter Sunday already implicit in Christmas Day, I think
> of you.

This remarkable letter is private and confessional, but it il-
luminates the less explicit mixture of Auden's homosexuality
and his Christian faith in many of his poems. Though the
letter draws upon a tradition of the intimate combination of
religious and erotic feeling in medieval and Renaissance poetry, the mixture has scandalized many critics of Auden's life
as well as his art. The sticking point is that Auden is speaking
unashamedly about his marriage and sexual relation to a man
rather than a woman. As Mendelson has remarked, however,
at the time he wrote the letter Auden regarded marriage, including his marriage to Kallman, as any "sexual relation governed by vows . . . an ethical and symbolic relation, not a legal
and economic one," and one that is "indifferent to the sexuality of the persons joined by it." Auden listed his turbulent response to Kallman's betrayal of their marriage as one of the
principal reasons for his return to the Anglican Church. But
another possible reason as well, as Auden's biographer Humphrey Carpenter has suggested, is that it was the marriage to
Kallman and its promise of a stable relation, one more free of
guilt about his homosexuality, that initially allowed him to
contemplate going back to the Church. Both these considerations help explain the emotional intensity, as well as the sad-

ness, of the letter, for it is an elegy, not an epithalamium. Auden and Kallman remained intimate friends for the rest of their lives and often lived together, but the relationship became more that of parent and child. They apparently were not again lovers.

There are many works at the turn of the decade that demonstrate a similar suffusion of Christian faith in Auden's emotional as well as intellectual life, including *The Prolific and the Devourer,* a long, unfinished work of prose written in early 1939, and *The Double Man,* which was written in 1940, though published a year later. In *The Prolific and the Devourer,* which he referred to in a letter as his "pensées," Auden began to explore the articles of his faith comprehensively. Writing in the shadow of a coming world war, Auden devotes the last section of the four-part work to a condemnation of violence and an assertion of his pacifism, though when the war came, he unhesitatingly tried to enlist in the U.S. military service and was rejected because of his homosexuality. The earlier sections of the work are devoted to more strictly theological issues, though with an underlying accent on social consciousness, on the need to love one's neighbor as oneself. This emphasis is most apparent in part 2, where Auden explains the truths of the Gospels in secular, and particularly physical, terms. "In using the terms Father and Son to express the relation of the divine and the human, rather than, say, King and subject," he writes, Christ "makes the relation a physical not an intellectual one, for it is precisely because in the relation of parent and child the physical material relation is so impossible to deny, that it is so difficult for a human parent not to love their children irrespective of their moral judgement." Similarly, in saying, "Thou shalt love thy neighbour as thyself," Auden remarks, "Again Jesus bases love on the most primitive instinct of all, self-preservation." He points out that "Jesus never said" that one should love one's neighbor *more* than thyself, "only the churches." "On the contrary," Auden continues, "at the last supper, he took eating, the most elementary and solitary act of all, the primary act of self-love, the only thing that not only man but all living creatures must do irrespective of species, sex, race or belief, and made it the symbol of universal love."

Auden always insisted on the material, the physical, ultimately all the realities and necessities of man's bodily condition, in human experience, and the proper understanding and acceptance of the flesh and its relation to the spirit was a central, if not the central, concern of his Christian faith as well as of his poetry. In a journal he kept in 1929 he noted that "Body and Soul (Not-Me and Me)" cannot exist independently, but they are nonetheless distinct, and that any effort to transform one into the other is destructive. He argued also that attempts to develop each individually have diminished rather than increased the capacity to love, on one hand, or to think, on the other. He added that loving one's neighbor "is a bodily, blood relationship," while developing the mind leads "away from nature" to increasing individualism and differentiation. "Only body," he concluded, "can be communicated." Much later in his life, in 1963, Auden moderated this statement, writing,

> Our bodies cannot love:
> But, without one,
> What works of Love could we do?

Behind the earlier analysis was Auden's tendency to see his own prodigal intellect as an alienating element in his relationships with others. The tendency was especially acute in 1929, when he was young, though it never entirely left him.

In 1940 Auden said that by rejecting as heresies both the Arian and Manichaean views of the relationship of mind and body, the Christian Church, in contrast to classical cultures, "was able to relate the universal to the particular, the spiritual to the material, and made the technical advance of civilization possible." In a later variant of this idea, Auden wrote in a letter to a priest in 1956 that "it does seem to me that the Doctrine of the Incarnation implies the coinherence of spirit and flesh in all creatures, and that materialism and manicheeism are mirror images of each other. (Between you and me, I feel that animals have more element of Spirit than St. Thomas allows them)." The stigmatization of matter and the body as evil by the Manichaeans preoccupied Auden throughout his life and was a major reason for his attraction to Saint Augustine, who had originally been a follower of Manichaeus but eventually and emphatically rejected his doctrines. Auden quoted Augustine's celebrated remark in the *Confessions,* "Make me chaste, Lord, but not yet," in his poem "The Love Feast."

In *The Prolific and the Devourer,* the opposition of body and mind seems to be the topic most important to Auden. At the outset of the work, he states that "all the striving of life is a striving to transcend duality, and establish unity or freedom," and in a significant passage almost immediately following he suggests his personal susceptibility to that duality: "At first the baby sees his limbs as belonging to the outside world. When he has learnt to control them, he accepts them as parts of himself. What we call the 'I,' in fact, is the area over which our will is immediately operative. Thus, if we have a toothache, we seem to be two people, the suffering 'I' and the hostile outer world of the tooth. His penis never fully belongs to a man." Auden often repeated this statement, including a version of it in verse that he published as a note to "New Year Letter" in *The Double Man.* There can be no question he meant it as a description of a Pauline division that exists in all men, but it is also clear that his own sense of division was emphatic and was a significant reason for his attraction to the rites of the liturgy. "Only in rites," he wrote at the end of his life, "can we renounce our oddities / and be truly entired."

It is clear as well that his sense of division was not just a function of his sexuality. His body was to some degree always a foreign object to Auden, despite his constant insistence upon it and his profound yearning to feel united with it. Robert Medley spoke of Auden's "innate physical clumsiness," and by Auden's own amused admission, as a schoolboy he was "mentally precocious, physically backward, short-sighted, a rabbit at all games, very untidy and grubby, a nail-biter, a physical coward." In a review in 1965, Auden noted that he had a "total lack of interest in and aptitude for games of any kind" at school but that he did not envy athletes, "because I knew that their skill could never be mine," and "I have always admired anybody who does something well." Nevertheless, in a draft of "The Sea and the Mirror" he spoke (in the character of Prospero) of the need to atone for "the humiliating performance in the gymnasium," and his conspicuous lack of care in his dress throughout his adult life accented both his body and his ungainliness. He remarked in a review that he was "one of those persons who generally look like an unmade bed," and in "Profile," he said of his clothes,

> The way he dresses
> reveals an angry baby,
> howling to be dressed.

In his later years Auden redefined and expanded the simple opposition between mind and body, the Me and Not-Me, that is found in his journal in 1929. He repeatedly objected to the failure to understand the scriptural idea of "the flesh," writing in 1954, for example, "It is unfortunate that the word 'Flesh,' set in contrast to 'Spirit,' is bound to suggest not what the Gospels and St. Paul intended it to mean, the whole physical-historical nature of fallen man, but his physical nature alone." In *A Certain World* in 1970 he wrote that in one of the new translations of the Bible that he found appalling, "the Greek word which St. Paul uses in Romans VIII and which the Authorized Version translates as *flesh* turns into *our lower nature*, a concept which is not Christian, but Manichean." But even with this inclusive understanding of the flesh, Auden could still say, late in his life, that it called for an act of faith to believe "that the Self of which I am aware and I are an indissoluble unity, for my immediate experience is of a Self, both physical and mental, which I am inhabiting like a house or driving like a motor-car." In a similar mood—he was capable of others—he wrote in "You,"

> Really, must you,
> Over-familiar
> Dense companion,
> Be there always?
> The bond between us
> Is chimerical surely:
> Yet I cannot break it.
>
> . . . .

Why am I certain,
Whatever your faults are,
The fault is mine,
Why is loneliness not
A chemical discomfort,
Nor Being a smell?

In *The Prolific and the Devourer* Auden states that "the false philosophy in all its forms starts out from a dualistic division between either The Whole and its parts, or one part of the whole and another. One part is good with absolute right to exist unchanged; the other is evil with no right to exist." "The dualism," he continues, "may be supernatural and theological, God and Satan; metaphysical, body and soul, energy and reason; or political, the philosopher king and the ignoble masses, the State and the individual, the proletariat and the masses." The origin of the false philosophy is the oversimplification and falsification of St. Paul's distinction between the flesh and the spirit, a subject upon which Auden was later to write at length. Auden asserts, following Saint Augustine, that "there are not 'good' and 'evil' existences. All existences are good, i.e. they are equally free and have an equal right to their existence. Everything that is is holy." Several years later, in an anonymous article in *The Commonweal* written after he had reaffirmed his faith, Auden related dualism to the Fall and argued that "if we cannot resolve the dualism of our experience, it is in our perception of existence that this dualism must lie, not in existence itself, i.e. a contradiction we manufacture for ourselves because we have eaten of the tree of the Knowledge of Good and Evil." Auden also says in *The Prolific and the Devourer* that "the animals, whose evolution is finished, i.e. whose knowledge of their relations to the rest of creation is fixed, can do evil, but they cannot sin. But we, being divided beings composed of a number of selves each with its false conception of its self-interest, sin in most that we do, for we rarely act in such a way that even the false self-interests of all our different selves are satisfied." "The majority of our actions," he continues, "are in the interest of one of these selves, not always the same one, at the expense of the rest. The consciousness that we are acting contrary to the interests of the others is our consciousness of sin, for to sin is consciously to act contrary to self-interest." That sin entails the consciousness of doing harm to oneself as well as others is a familiar Christian concept; what Auden characteristically adds is that because of the inescapable dualism of man's fallen nature, sin exacerbates human self-division. Auden habitually celebrated the unity of being that animals enjoy because of their freedom from consciousness.

The sense of self-division never left Auden, and both before and after the renewal of his faith, dualism remained an active part of his imagination. But his insistence that in this world "all experience is dualistic" had positive as well as negative inflections. At one extreme, contemplating the destruction of World War II as well as the threat of the Cold War and the new atomic age in 1950, he could declare with Augustinian rhetoric that "the dualism inaugurated by Luther, Machiavelli, and Descartes has brought us to the end of our tether and we know that either we must discover a unity which can repair the fissures that separate the individual from society, feeling from intellect, and conscience from both, or we shall surely die by spiritual despair and physical annihilation." In a celebrated line in "September 1, 1939," he had said more simply, but analogously, "We must love one another or die." But he also could write, more hopefully, "Man is neither pure spirit nor pure nature—if he were purely either he would have no history—but exists in and as a tension between their two opposing polarities." In a review of Carl Sandburg's biography of Abraham Lincoln, he accordingly praised what he called "binocular vision" and said that the "one infallible symptom of greatness is the capacity for double focus."

Auden wrote of double focus and dualism again in *The Double Man*, an encyclopedic work consisting of a verse prologue and epilogue; a long verse epistle, accompanied by an extensive mixture of prose and verse notes, entitled "New Year Letter"; and an extended sonnet sequence entitled "The Quest." The epigraph of the work is drawn from Montaigne's "Of Glorie": "We are, I know not how, double in ourselves, so that what we believe we disbelieve, and cannot rid ourselves of what we condemn"; and in "New Year Letter" Auden calls "the gift of double focus / That magic lamp" that "Can be a sesame to light," and sees it as a remedy against the Devil, "the great schismatic who / First split creation into two," "who controls / The moral asymmetric souls / The either-ors, the mongrel halves / Who find truth in a mirror."

The moral asymmetries Auden confronted in the world of 1940 in "New Year Letter" were extreme:

> The Asiatic cry of pain,
> The shots of executing Spain . . .
> The dazed uncomprehending stare
> Of the Danubian despair,
> The Jew wrecked in the German cell,
> Flat Poland frozen into hell.

The quest to understand the evil in this world in the context of Christian belief is incipient throughout "New Year Letter" and is indeed its goal, though it becomes especially apparent in the later portions of the poem and in the notes, which Auden composed as his formal religious commitment was crystallizing. "New Year Letter" is filled with overt biblical and Christian references and allusions. It dismisses the "Gnostics in the brothels," for example, for "treating / The flesh as secular and fleeting," a heresy which, Auden wrote in a letter, he found "false and repellant." It alludes to, and in its notes quotes extensively from, Dante's "Purgatorio," Pascal's *Pensées,* Kierkegaard's *Journals,* and Paul Tillich's *The Interpretation of History,* among other religious texts. In another note Auden indicates that "the source of many ideas" in the poem was Williams's *The Descent of the Dove,* and other notes include brief verses by Auden himself on such subjects as Luther's faith and Montaigne's doubt. The final note is a poem on the Incarnation. In addition, in passages in "New Year Letter" otherwise reproduced verbatim from *The Prolific and the Devourer,* there are small but critical changes that make the underlying Christian faith of the earlier work more explicit. The "false philosophy" of dualism in *The Prolific and the Devourer,* for example, becomes "the Devil's philosophy" in a note to "New Year Letter," and the discussion of dualism in both the poem and notes is placed in the context of a larger consideration of how the Devil paradoxically serves God's purposes. In another passage, pointed out by Mendelson, Auden simply adds the word "God" to a passage from the earlier work in which God is intimated but not named.

The most crucial of the Christian references in "New Year Letter," however, occur in the prayer that makes up the penultimate stanza:

O Unicorn among the cedars,
To whom no magic charm can lead us,
White childhood moving like a sigh
Through the green woods unharmed in thy
Sophisticated innocence,
To call thy true love to the dance,
O Dove of science and of light . . .
Send strength sufficient for our day,
And point our knowledge on its way,
O da quod jubes, Domine.

The association of the unicorn and the dove with Christ is traditional; the child and the dance have paradisal associations for Auden; and there is a revealing couplet in the draft that Auden omitted in the printed version, "O order the electrons sing / Dancing in their atomic ring," that relates science to the ring of agape. But the most telling of the Christian references is the quotation from Augustine's *Confessions,* which Auden may have drawn from Williams's *The Descent of the Dove:* "*O da quod jubes*" [O give what thou commandest]. The context of the statement in the *Confessions* is, "Give what thou commandest, and command what thou wilt. Thou imposest continency upon us; and when I perceived, as one saith, that no man can be continent unless thou give it, this also was a point of wisdom, to know whose gift it was." Pelagius attacked this statement and contended that man could take the fundamental steps toward salvation by his own efforts, apart from the assistance of Divine Grace. In the controversy with the Pelagians that occupied the last part of his life, Augustine maintained, on the contrary, that man had an absolute need for God's Grace, since his will itself had become corrupted at

the Fall. The issues involved in the controversy—the Fall,
Original Sin, and Predestination—were fundamental, and Augustine's association of them with sexual continence had particular cogency for Auden. He wrote in a review at the time
he was composing the poem, "Even Augustine who said 'O
Thou who commandest Chastity, give what Thou commandest' was not denying free-will, but only saying that in order to
will you must first believe that you can."

"New Year Letter" closes with a personal prayer. In its
final stanza, Auden praises Elizabeth Mayer, "Dear friend
Elizabeth, dear friend," the person to whom he has addressed
the entire epistle:

> We fall down in the dance, we make
> The old ridiculous mistake,
> But always there are such as you
> Forgiving, helping what we do.
> O every day in sleep and labor
> Our life and death are with our neighbor.

"Our life and death are with our neighbor" adapts Saint Ath-
anasius's "Your life and death are with your neighbor," which
Williams also quotes in *The Descent of the Dove* and which,
along with the need for forgiveness, are focal points of Auden's faith.

"The Quest," the twenty sonnets that follow "New Year
Letter" in *The Double Man,* is Auden's modern version of the
epic or romantic quest for the Holy Grail. The sequence constitutes a search for a self which can find its integrity in faith,
and it deals with many religious subjects, including sonnets
on the three temptations of Christ as well as on a number of
religious themes developed by Kierkegaard. The culminating
point of the sequence, the sonnet that crystallizes its entire

movement, is the final one, "The Garden." It evokes the paradisal garden as well as the garden in which Augustine was
converted to Christianity, the garden in which, as Williams
wrote in a phrase that Auden echoes, "the universe for Augustine had shifted its centre":

> Within these gates all opening begins:
> White shouts and flickers through its green and red,
> Where children play at seven earnest sins
> And dogs believe their tall conditions dead.
>
> Here adolescence into number breaks
> The perfect circle time can draw on stone,
> And flesh forgives division as it makes
> Another moment of consent its own.
>
> All journeys die here: wish and weight are lifted . . .
>
> The gaunt and great, the famed for conversation
> Blushed in the stare of evening as they spoke,
> And felt their centre of volition shifted.

All the familiar features of paradise in Auden's imagination
are present in this poem: the innocent children playing, not
yet susceptible to sin; the green garden; the light; the perfect
circle of time; the grace that transforms the will; and above
all, the forgiveness of duality. "And flesh forgives division as it
makes / Another moment of consent its own" could be considered a description of the central struggle of Auden's inner
life; it is certainly the epigraph for his return to the Church.

In the epilogue to *The Double Man,* which contemplates
"the darkness of tribulation and death," Auden associates
grace, "the knowledge that we must know to will," explicitly
with "Jesus," the first time, as Mendelson points out, he
names Jesus in his poetry, though he had named him often in

his prose. The final stanza of the epilogue expresses a hope for the resolution of duality and of the Manichaean conflict of light and dark, offering a prayer that

> the shabby structure of indolent flesh
> give a resonant echo to the Word which was
> from the beginning, and the shining
> Light be comprehended by the darkness.

These lines are themselves a resonant echo, of the first chapter of John, in which while "the light of men . . . shineth in darkness; and the darkness comprehended it not," John, proclaiming that "the Word was made Flesh and dwelt among us," bears witness to "the true Light, which lighteth every man that cometh into the world."

CHAPTER TWO

For the Time Being

The volume entitled *For the Time Being*, which was published in 1944, consists of "For the Time Being," which Auden began writing towards the end of 1941 and finished in July 1942, and *The Sea and the Mirror*, which he wrote from October 1942 to February 1944, while he was teaching at Swarthmore College. Auden placed "For the Time Being" last in the volume, though he wrote it first, because he thought that the secular, if religiously informed, exploration of art in *The Sea and the Mirror* should be a prelude to the manifestly religious representation of the Incarnation in "For the Time Being."

"For the Time Being"

Auden dedicated "For the Time Being" to his mother, Constance Bicknell Auden, who had died in the summer of

1941, and with whom his faith had always been deeply intertwined. In the *Confessions,* Augustine mentions that he devoutly drank in the name of God "even together with my mother's milk," and Auden might have said the same. As John Fuller observes, "For the Time Being" is "suffused with an eagerness to make the sort of difficult peace with the Flesh (and, interestingly enough, peace with the mother) that is found in Augustine's *Confessions.*"

The subtitle of "For the Time Being" is "A Christmas Oratorio," and Auden initially intended the work to be set to music by Benjamin Britten. But though the poem conforms to the structure of an oratorio, it also has affinities with the medieval mystery play. Essentially a drama of the Incarnation, of the Word made Flesh, the mystery, or craft, cycles enacted the events of biblical history from Creation to Doomsday within a secular, and often comic, story in order to make religious history understandable in terms of ordinary human experience. The plays were performed by amateur groups made up of townspeople, frequently craft guilds appropriate to particular episodes (Noah's flood, for example, would be performed by the shipwright's guild), who were recognizable to their audience as their contemporaries, dressed in the same clothes and sharing the same everyday existence. The events were presented, as in the liturgy, as eternally recurrent, and episodes of the Old Testament were understood as prefigurations of the New. The mystery drama was likely to have originated in the Feast of Corpus Christi, in which the Eucharist was led in procession from the altar of the church into the marketplace of the town, manifesting the presence of Christ in the daily lives of the townspeople.

Auden conceived of "For the Time Being"—as he conceived of religious faith in his own life—in just this way, as he
made clear in a letter explaining the work to his father. "Sorry
you are puzzled by the Oratorio," he wrote in the letter:

> Perhaps you were expecting a purely historical account as
> one might give of the battle of Waterloo, whereas I was try-
> ing to treat it as a religious event which eternally recurs
> every time it is accepted. Thus the historical fact that the
> shepherds were *shepherds* is religiously accidental—the
> religious fact is that they were the poor and humble of this
> world for which at this moment the historical expression is
> the city-proletariat, and so on with all the other figures. . . .
>
> I am not the first to treat the Christian data in this way;
> until the 18th Cent. it was always done, in the Mystery
> Plays for instance or any Italian paintings. It is only in the
> last two centuries that religion has been "humanised," and
> therefore treated historically as something that happened a
> long time ago; hence the nursery picture of Jesus in a night-
> gown and a Parsifal beard.
>
> If a return to the older method now seems more star-
> tling it is partly because of the acceleration in the rate of
> historical change due to industrialization—there is a far
> greater difference between the accidents of life in 1600 AD
> and in 1942 than between those of 30 AD and 1600.

Auden returned to these ideas many years later, in a manuscript note that was probably intended to be a commentary
for the broadcast of parts of "For the Time Being" on Austrian television in 1967. "Anyone who attempts to use" a sacred historical event "as a theme for a work of art," he wrote
in the manuscript, "has to do justice both to the historicity of
the event and to its contemporary relevance. This is not easy.

If, in treating the Christmas story, he writes as a secular historian would, ie, he makes the clothes, the architecture, the dialogue as nearly what they actually were in Palestine during the reign of Augustus as scholarship can bring them, his piece will, for a twentieth century audience, be simply an archeological curiosity." On the other hand, if "he makes all his properties and imagery contemporary, the story ceases to be one which the audience are required to believe really happened, and becomes an entertaining myth."

"For the Time Being" does not consistently achieve the balance Auden describes, and perhaps for that reason, though the poem remains a standard and compelling text for believing Christians, its literary quality is uneven. Many sections, the early choruses and most of the early narrations, for example, appear to be largely dutiful recitations, as opposed to those like "The Temptation of Joseph" and the depiction of Herod in "The Massacre of the Innocents," which richly combine historicity and contemporary urgency and in which, not coincidentally, Auden is clearly enjoying himself. "For the Time Being" also proved to be far too long and intricate to serve Auden's original conception of it as a libretto for an oratorio, and the absence of music perhaps leaves some of its less inspired sections more exposed. In addition, the highly familiar details of the biblical narrative that subsumes "For the Time Being" may have inhibited Auden in this instance. The much less well-known background of *The Tempest* that informs *The Sea and the Mirror* had a more sustained and liberating effect on his imagination.

"The Temptation of St. Joseph," in any event, the portrayal of Joseph's response to Mary's birth of the Child, is the first section in the poem that fully reveals both the richness of

Auden's characteristic voice and the comic contemporaneity
of the mystery drama. It begins with Joseph speaking:

> My shoes were shined, my pants were cleaned
> and pressed,
> And I was hurrying to meet
> My own true Love.

The Chorus comments,

> *Joseph, you have heard*
> *What Mary says occurred;*
> *Yes, it may be so.*
> *Is it likely? No.*

The succeeding two choruses are similar. The second says,

> *Mary may be pure,*
> *But, Joseph, are you sure?*
> *How is one to tell?*
> *Suppose, for instance . . . Well . . .*

The Chorus's last comment is,

> *Maybe not, maybe not.*
> *But Joseph, you know what*
> *Your world, of course, will say*
> *About you anyway.*

The depiction of Joseph's feelings of "cuckoldry" is at
once scandalously comic and serious, and its effect is incisive.
Because it voices an ordinary human reaction to Mary's preg-
nancy, considered biologically rather than, as the Gospels treat
it, as a mystery and miracle, it encourages readers to become
involved in Auden's own dialectic of skepticism and faith. It
may also be particularly compelling for Christian readers because it invites them to think about their own reactions to a

Christmas story they have been told to accept without debate since early childhood.

"The Temptation of Joseph" is in the first instance autobiographical, a representation of Auden's own painful feelings about Chester Kallman's betrayal of the relationship that Auden had considered a marriage. He told Alan Ansen, his secretary and friend, "Joseph is me," and in a letter to Ansen he also listed "The Temptation of St. Joseph" as one of a number of works connected to what he called "l'affaire C." Auden's identification with Joseph, however, was more than simply autobiographical. Auden was also unusually hostile to the doctrines of the Virgin Birth and of the Immaculate Conception. In an interview near the end of his life with John Bridgen, an Anglican clergyman, Auden remarked of the Virgin Birth, "What does it say but that no-one can acknowledge that his parents had sex!"; and under the heading of "Conception, The Immaculate" in *A Certain World,* he wrote, "Behind this ingenious doctrine lies, I cannot help suspecting, a not very savory wish to make the Mother of God an Honorary Gentile. As if we didn't all know perfectly well that the Holy Ghost and Our Lady both speak British English, He with an Oxford, She with a Yiddish, accent." Auden made these objections often. His brother John, for example, noted that there were "dogmas to which Wystan took strong exception; the Immaculate Conception in his view making an Honorary Aryan of the Blessed Virgin, a bizarre idea which he repeated every time we met." Since John "went over to Rome in 1951," one may easily imagine Auden taking delight in repeating it to him.

The serious source of Auden's objections to both doctrines, however, was his antipathy to any attempt to deny the

biological reality of human existence and his corresponding desire to affirm the importance of the body. It is of great significance that he should have described the liturgy as "the rites of public worship in which we bring our bodies to God." He eventually criticized Kierkegaard for failing to recognize "that human beings are not ghosts but have bodies of flesh and blood." "As a spirit, a conscious person endowed with free will," Auden wrote, "every man has, through faith and grace, a unique 'existential' relation to God, and few since St. Augustine have described this relation more profoundly than Kierkegaard." "But every man," Auden insisted, "has a second relation to God which is neither unique nor existential: as a creature composed of matter, as a biological organism, every man, in common with everything else in the universe, is related by necessity to the God who created that universe and saw that it was good, for the laws of nature to which, whether he likes it or not, he must conform are of divine origin." In another essay, in which he also reassessed Kierkegaard, Auden quoted Dietrich Bonhoeffer's observation that "to long for the transcendent when you are in your wife's arms is, to put it mildly, a lack of taste and it is certainly not what God expects of us." In his interview with Bridgen, Auden said from a different perspective, but to the same effect, "Sexuality is only truly appreciated within a loving relationship. 'Be fruitful and multiply' says Genesis but gives as the primary reason for the sexes, 'It is not good that man should be alone.' By contrast all pornography is Manichaean. Its purpose is to throw shame on the bodily functions." Auden could never endorse the shaming of such functions, and there is a strong anti-Manichaean subtext in his sympathetic identification with Joseph.

Auden also makes Joseph's predicament a test for the Kierkegaardian leap of faith. With a suffering that is palpably Auden's own, he depicts Joseph "Caught in the jealous trap / Of an empty house," sitting "alone in the dark," and when Joseph asks for

> one
> Important and elegant proof
> That what my Love had done
> Was really at your will
> And that your will is Love,

Gabriel answers only that he "must believe."

In a further turn of Joseph's temptation, a narrator says that his suffering is a necessary atonement

> For the perpetual excuse
> Of Adam for his fall—"My little Eve,
> God bless her, did beguile me and I ate,"
>   For his insistence on a nurse,
> All service, breast, and lap, for giving Fate
> Feminine gender to make girls believe
> That they can save him, you must now atone,
>   Joseph, in silence and alone.

The narrator proceeds to recite a long list of masculine conceits, many of them, as Fuller remarks, Thurberesque, and concludes by stating, "There is one World of Nature and one Life; / Sin fractures the Vision, not the Fact. . . . To choose what is difficult all one's days / As if it were easy, that is faith. Joseph, praise." That was Auden's own view, and not only of his experience with Kallman. The blending of unyielding comedy, suffering, and humility in "The Temptation of St. Joseph" is extraordinary.

A subsequent section of the poem includes a lullaby in which Mary says to the Child, in a stanza that characteristically focuses on the flesh,

> Sleep. What have you learned from the womb that bore
> you
> But an anxiety your Father cannot feel?
> Sleep. What will the flesh that I gave do for you,
> Or my mother's love, but tempt you from His will?
> Why was I chosen to teach His Son to weep?
> Little One, sleep.

Mary's maternal love for the Christ Child heightens the consciousness of His existence in the flesh, and in this context the denial of anxiety in the Father further accents the Child's humanity. Later in his life Auden changed his mind about the Father's remoteness and adopted the Patripassion heresy, which states that the Father shared Christ's human anxiety and grief.

In "The Meditation of Simeon," the central prose section of "For the Time Being," Auden explores the theological meaning of the Incarnation in detail. He wrote his father that Simeon's meditation "gives a theological interpretation of why the Incarnation took place historically when it did, and what difference it makes to our feeling and thinking." Auden's historical understanding of the Incarnation was influenced by Charles Norris Cochrane's *Christianity and Classical Culture,* a book he read in 1940 and whose revised edition he reviewed admiringly in 1944. Cochrane argued that Christianity, particularly Saint Augustine's synthesis of it, properly diagnosed, if it did not immediately heal, the spiritual breakdown of classical culture. Recapitulating Cochrane's thesis in a review of

Reinhold Niebuhr's *The Nature and Destiny of Man* in 1941,
Auden wrote that the Incarnation "occurred precisely at that
moment in history when an impasse seemed to have been
reached. The civilized world was now politically united, but
its philosophical dualism divided both society and the individual personality horizontally, the wise from the ignorant,
the Logos from the Flesh; the only people who did not do this
were the Jews, but they divided society vertically, themselves
from the rest of the world." "The Incarnation," Auden continued, "asserts that at an actual moment in historical time,
the Word was actually made Flesh, the possibility of the
union of the finite with the infinite made a fact."

In "The Meditation of Simeon," Simeon rehearses a number of the dilemmas of classical culture that led to the Incarnation, including the dualism of "the One and the Many," the
difficulty of reconciling unity and diversity, and the impossibility of man's becoming conscious of Original Sin, "because
it is itself what conditions his will to knowledge." In a passage
describing the Incarnation that Auden had significantly revised, Simeon says, "But here and now the Word which is implicit in the Beginning and in the End is become immediately
explicit, and that which hitherto we could only passively fear
as the incomprehensible I AM, henceforth we may actively
love with comprehension that THOU ART." In the first edition of the poem, Auden had written "HE IS" instead of
"THOU ART." The striking revision to "THOU ART" in
later editions derives from Auden's reading of Martin Buber's
I and Thou, a work of Jewish theology that was celebrated at
the time by many Protestant theologians, including Niebuhr.
The relationship of love, Buber wrote in *I and Thou,* is "usually understood wrongly as being one of feeling. Feelings ac-

company the metaphysical and metapsychical fact of love, but they do not constitute it. . . . The feeling of Jesus for the demoniac differs from his feeling for the beloved disciple; but the love is the one love. Feelings are 'entertained': love comes to pass. Feelings dwell in man; but man dwells in his love. . . . Love is responsibility of an *I* for a *Thou*." Buber distinguished two kinds of relations in human life: I-it relations, in which the self is related to things and to people perceived only as things, and I-Thou relations, in which the I's whole being is fully realized through a dialogue with God, the "eternal Thou," and in consequence with the "Thous" of his fellow human beings as well. To make the it a Thou, Buber asserted, requires unceasing effort: "Between you and it there is mutual giving: you say *Thou* to it and give yourself to it, it says *Thou* to you and gives itself to you. . . . Through the graciousness of its comings and the solemn sadness of its goings it leads you away to the *Thou* in which the parallel lines of relations meet." For Auden, this was a deeply compelling way of understanding both the love of one's neighbor as oneself and the love of God, and it was consonant as well with his own sense of the simultaneous depth and evanescence of visionary experience. In addition, Buber's Kierkegaardian focus on the individual's existential relation to God, his interest in the historical and the concrete, and above all his sanctification of daily life were equally in harmony with Auden's own religious beliefs as well as with his immediate purposes in "For the Time Being." Buber's epigraph to *I and Thou*, taken from Goethe, was "So, waiting, I have won from you the ends / God's presence in each element."

In the final part of his meditation, Simeon considers the effect of the Incarnation upon science as well as art. He says

of science that because of the union of the Word and flesh
"without loss of perfection," reason can be "redeemed from
incestuous fixation on her own Logic"; the general need not
be opposed to the particular; the one and the many can be
"simultaneously revealed as real"; and "the continuous development of Science" is assured. Auden's belief that Christianity promoted the growth of science, rather than threatened
it, was characteristic of both his temperament and thought.
He maintained that scientific formulations had more to fear
from "a naturalistic religion like Marxism" than from Christianity, and although he was hardly a logical positivist, he had,
as Isherwood claimed, a scientific disposition that was unusual for a poet. He wrote in 1953 that

> it's as well at times
> To be reminded that nothing is lovely,
> Not even in poetry, which is not the case.

In 1964 he said, "It is impossible for something to be true
for one mind and false for another. That is to say, if two of us
disagree, either one of us is right or both of us are wrong."
In 1968 he said that "abhorred in the Heav'ns are all / self-
proclaimed poets who, to wow an / audience, utter some resonant lie"; and in a lecture he said that "our hearts as well as
our intellects are corrupted when we use words for purposes
to which the judgement true/or/false is irrelevant." In *A Certain World* in 1970, he wrote, "I cannot accept the doctrine
that in poetry there is a 'suspension of belief.' A poet must
never make a statement simply because it sounds poetically
exciting; he must also believe it to be true." These premises
are evident in Auden's frequent radical revisions of some of
his poems as well as in his exclusions of others from his canon,

when he decided he could no longer believe that something he had written was true. Though critics have regretted or disputed both the revisions and the exclusions, it is important, whatever one's opinion, to bear in mind how much these kinds of changes were basic to Auden's conception of poetry as well as his practice of it.

Simeon's explanation of the effect of the Incarnation upon art, which "For the Time Being" itself embodies, if only partly, has the most immediate bearing on Auden's own work. "Because in Him," Simeon says, "the Flesh is united to the Word without magical transformation, Imagination is redeemed from promiscuous fornication with her own images. The tragic conflict of Virtue with Necessity is no longer confined to the Exceptional Hero; for disaster is not the impact of a curse upon a few great families, but issues continually from the hubris of every tainted will." "Every invalid," Simeon suggests, "is Roland defending the narrow pass against hopeless odds, every stenographer Brünnhilde refusing to renounce her lover's ring which came into existence through the renunciation of love." Like Augustine, Auden was always suspicious of art's pretension to magical transformations— "promiscuous fornication with her own images" refers to Augustine's *fantastica fornicatio*, the prostitution of the mind to its own fantasies. The liturgy, on the contrary, can effect transformation without magic. Auden entitled one of his lectures honoring T. S. Eliot in 1967 "Words and the Word," and the distinction between the two was absolute for him. He never treated the liturgy as a work of art, however susceptible he might have been as a boy and as a man to its "exciting magical rites" and its aesthetic properties.

Simeon also considers the effect of the Incarnation upon

comedy. "Nor is the Ridiculous," he says, "a species any longer of the Ugly; for since of themselves all men are without merit, all are ironically assisted to their comic bewilderment by the Grace of God." "Nor is there any situation," Simeon says further, "which is essentially more or less interesting than another. Every tea-table is a battlefield littered with old catastrophes and haunted by the vague ghosts of vast issues, every martyrdom an occasion for flip cracks and sententious oratory." Auden repeated these ideas in a review of a book on James Joyce and Richard Wagner in which he discussed the changes that the advent of Christianity and the conception of original sin brought to the subject matter of pagan literature: "Instead of the artist being confined to the over-life-size," he wrote, "the melodramatic character and situation, any character or situation was artistically interesting that could show spiritual growth or decay; what mattered was the intensity of effort with relation to the capacity of a given character to make it: Christianity introduced the tea-table into literature."

This religious understanding of the "tea-table," which informed the mystery drama, also underlies the most successful verse in "For the Time Being" itself—and much of Auden's other work as well—and is apparent in his characterization not only of Joseph, but also of Herod. In the mystery plays Herod is portrayed comically as a raging tyrant; in the section entitled "The Massacre of the Innocents," Auden inverts the stereotype by portraying his Herod as all too rational. Auden wrote in his letter to his father that "what we know of Herod . . . is that he was a Hellenised-Jew and a political ruler. Accordingly I have made him express the intellectual's eternal objection to Christianity—that it replaces objectivity by subjectivity, and the politician's eternal objection that it regards the state as having only a negative role (See Marcus Aurelius)." In "For the Time Being" Herod thus says plaintively, "There is no visible disorder. No crime—what could be more innocent than the birth of an artisan's child? . . . Barges are unloading soil fertiliser at the river wharves. Soft drinks and sandwiches may be had in the inns at reasonable prices. . . . the truck-drivers no longer carry guns. Things are beginning to take shape." But even so, Herod says, superstition persists, "the captain of my own guard wears an amulet against the Evil Eye, and the richest merchant in the city consults a medium over every important transaction." And this, Herod complains, despite his prohibition of "the sale of crystals and ouija-boards," and a statute making it an offense "to turn tables or feel bumps."

"To-day apparently," Herod continues, "judging by the trio who came to see me this morning with an ecstatic grin on their scholarly faces, the job has been done. 'God has been born,' they cried, 'we have seen him ourselves. The World is saved. Nothing else matters.'" "One needn't be much of a psychologist," Herod comments, "to realize that if this rumour is not stamped out now, in a few years it is capable of diseasing the whole Empire." Among the inevitable consequences, he protests, "Reason will be replaced by Revelation. . . . Knowledge will degenerate into a riot of subjective visions—feelings in the solar plexus induced by undernourishment, angelic images generated by fevers or drugs, dream warnings inspired by the sound of falling water." Furthermore, he says, "Justice will be replaced by Pity as the cardinal human virtue, and all fear of retribution will vanish. Every corner-boy will congratulate himself: 'I'm such a sinner that God had to come

down in person to save me. I must be a devil of a fellow.'"
"Naturally," Herod concludes, "this cannot be allowed to hap-
pen," and then protests: "Why couldn't this wretched infant
be born somewhere else? Why can't people be sensible? . . .
Why can't they see that the notion of a finite God is absurd?
Because it is."

But suppose, he says, "just for the sake of argument," that
it is not, "that this story is true, that this child is in some inex-
plicable manner both God and Man, that he grows up, lives,
and dies, without committing a single sin? Would that make
life any better? On the contrary it would make it far, far
worse. For it could only mean this; that once having shown
them how, God would expect every man, whatever his fortune, to lead a sinless life in the flesh and on earth. Then indeed would the human race be plunged into madness and despair." Finally, complaining that personally "it would mean
that God had given me the power to destroy Himself," he
protests, "Why should He dislike me so? I've worked like a
slave. Ask anyone you like. I read all official dispatches without skipping. I've taken elocution lessons. I've hardly ever
taken bribes. How dare He allow me to decide? I've tried to
be good. I brush my teeth every night. I haven't had sex for
a month. I object. I'm a liberal. I want everyone to be happy.
I wish I had never been born."

Beneath the humor of Herod's petulant rational liberalism
lies a serious outline of the development of religious belief
from animism to natural and then revealed religion that Auden
had developed in *The Prolific and the Devourer* and his essays
in *The Commonweal.* Herod, of course, shows no understanding of forgiveness and redemption in his account of the consequences of the Incarnation, but he does consider Chris-

tianity, as Auden did, as a Way rather than a state. The speech, in addition, reflects Auden's belief that faith is at once absurd and a means of understanding everyday human experience.

Following Herod's speech is an adaptation of another staple of the mystery play, a brief verse section portraying a comic soldier: *"George, you old Emperor, / How did you get in the Army?"* The camp verses on George are followed by two sections devoted to Mary's and Joseph's "Flight Into Egypt," which include landscapes of decadence and desolation Auden was to revisit in *The Sea and the Mirror.* Finally, there is a narration, now wholly in the present, of the day after Christmas, when the tree must be dismantled, the decorations put back in their boxes, the holly and mistletoe taken down, and the children got ready for school:

> Once again
> As in previous years we have seen the actual Vision and
>   failed
> To do more than entertain it as an agreeable
> Possibility, once again we have sent Him away,
> Begging though to remain His disobedient servant,
> The promising child who cannot keep His word for long.

With the Christmas Feast "already a fading memory," the narrator says,

> already the mind begins to be vaguely aware
> Of an unpleasant whiff of apprehension at the thought
> Of Lent and Good Friday which cannot, after all, now
> Be very far off. But, for the time being, here we all are.

"To those who have seen / The Child," he adds, "however dimly, however incredulously, / The Time Being is, in a sense, the most trying time of all." He concludes,

>   The happy morning is over,
> The night of agony still to come; the time is noon:
> When the Spirit must practise his scales of rejoicing
> Without even a hostile audience, and the Soul endure
> A silence that is neither for nor against her faith
> That God's Will will be done, that, in spite of her prayers,
> God will cheat no one, not even the world of its triumph.

The last line is a paraphrase of an aphorism from Franz Kafka: "One must not cheat anybody, not even the world of its triumph." (Auden later, in a lecture on Shakespeare, cited a related aphorism by Kafka on the inescapability of suffering in the world.) In a letter to Theodore Spencer, a Harvard professor and friend to whom he often looked for criticism of his work in the 1940s, Auden said of the post-Christmas narration, "The Light may shine in darkness but to us its light is hid, because we have sent it away, i.e. the immediate post-Christmas temptation is that of the emotional let-down of an intense experience which is then suddenly over."

The final section of "For the Time Being" is a short and exultant Chorus. Auden wrote Spencer, "I tried to introduce the sweeter note in the last section, i.e. if the light is to be seen again, it is by going forward (to the Passion perhaps) and not by nostalgic reminiscence. One cannot *be* a little child; one has *to become* like one, and to do that one has to leave home, to lose even what now seems most good." The words of the Chorus are

> He is the Way.
> Follow Him through the Land of Unlikeness;
> You will see rare beasts, and have unique adventures.
>
> He is the Truth.
> Seek him in the Kingdom of Anxiety;

You will come to a great city that has expected your
   return for years.

He is the Life.
Love Him in the World of the Flesh;
And at your marriage all its occasions shall dance for joy.

The "Land of Unlikeness" is derived from Augustine's *Confessions:* "I found myself to be a long way from thee in the region of unlikeness [*in regione dissimilitudinis*]." All three stanzas suggest the vectors of Auden's faith, the achievement of the City of God on earth, the love of the Word made Flesh understood in the world of the flesh, in "the Kingdom of Anxiety." The celebratory final line resonates with an anonymous verse he was to quote in his commonplace book *A Certain World*, under the heading "Marriage":

> *Wenn der Rabbi trennt*
> *Schocklen sich die Wend*
> *Und alle Hassidim*
> *Kleppen mit die Hend.*

(When the Rabbi has marital intercourse, the walls shake, and all the Hassidim clap their hands.)

The Sea and the Mirror

Auden wrote in a letter to Ursula Niebuhr in June 1942 that *The Sea and the Mirror* "is really about the Christian conception of art," and in *The Commonweal* in November 1942 he said, "As a writer, who is also a would-be Christian, I cannot help feeling that a satisfactory theory of Art from the standpoint of the Christian faith has yet to be worked out." *The Sea and the Mirror: A Commentary on Shakespeare's*

"*The Tempest*" constitutes Auden's attempt, with the example of *The Tempest,* to work out that theory.

The action of the poem takes place after the curtain has fallen on a performance of Shakespeare's play. Auden was drawn to *The Tempest* in part because, like many critics before and since, he understood it as a skeptical work. He wrote Spencer that *The Sea and the Mirror* "is my Ars Poetica, in the same way I believe *The Tempest* to be Shakespeare's, ie I am attempting something which in a way is absurd, to show in a work of art, the limitations of art." In the concluding lecture of his year-long course on Shakespeare's works at the New School, Auden especially praised Shakespeare for his consciousness of these limitations: "There's something a little irritating in the determination of the very greatest artists, like Dante, Joyce, Milton, to create masterpieces and to think themselves important. To be able to devote one's life to art without forgetting that art is frivolous is a tremendous achievement of personal character. Shakespeare never takes himself too seriously."

The central limit of art that Shakespeare deals with in *The Tempest,* and that Auden explores in *The Sea and the Mirror,* is that art is doubly illusory because it holds the mirror up to nature rather than to the truth that passes human understanding. In *The Tempest,* a play that from first to last presents itself as an illusion of an illusion, Prospero renounces his art, and in the epilogue his renunciation is explicitly associated with the spiritual reality represented in the Lord's Prayer:

> Now I want
> Spirits to enforce, art to enchant;
> And my ending is despair
> Unless I be reliev'd by prayer,

Which pierces so that it assaults
Mercy itself and frees all faults.
As you from crimes would pardon'd be,
Let your indulgence set me free.

The Tempest's exploration of the limits of art is enacted within a dualistic, allegorical structure, with Prospero as well as most of the rest of the cast poised between the animalistic representation of Caliban and the nonhuman figure of Ariel, the former variously interpreted by critics as nature, the flesh, the id, the latter as the immaterial, the spirit, the imagination. Auden's active interest in Augustine at the time made him especially susceptible to this opposition in the play. He wrote to Stephen Spender in 1942 that he had "been reading St Augustine a lot lately who is quite wonderful," and he took notes on the *Confessions* at the end of the notebook in which he drafted "For the Time Being" and parts of *The Sea and the Mirror*. The *Confessions* is reflected not only in a number of important details in *The Sea and the Mirror,* particularly in Prospero's speech, but also in Auden's broader identification in the poem with Augustine's fundamental rejection of Manichaeism's dichotomy of Spirit and Flesh, as well as with his objections to the presumptions of rhetoric. In an essay on *The Tempest* written in 1954, Auden said, "As a biological organism Man is a natural creature subject to the necessities of nature; as a being with consciousness and will, he is at the same time a historical person with the freedom of the spirit. *The Tempest* seems to me a manichean work, not because it shows the relation of Nature to Spirit as one of conflict and hostility, which in fallen man it is, but because it puts the blame for this upon Nature and makes the Spirit innocent."

Though Auden objected to what he considered Shakespeare's Manichaean opposition of Ariel and Caliban and its consequent spiritual elevation of Prospero's art, the schematic dualism itself was, as always, compelling to him and may have been one of the main reasons he chose to adapt *The Tempest*. Caliban is in constant counterpoint with Ariel in *The Tempest*—they cannot be imagined without each other—and their opposition informs or reflects everything else in the play. Antonio and Sebastian's unregenerate rapaciousness and desperation contrast throughout with Gonzalo's beneficence and hopefulness. Venus is counterpointed with Ceres within the wedding masque, and the conspiracy of Caliban, Stephano, and Trinculo complements as well as disrupts the performance of the masque, the high artifice and graciousness of which remain in our memory as much as the drunken malice of the conspiracy remains in Prospero's. Similarly, Miranda's celebrated lines, "O brave new world / That has such people in't," coexist with Prospero's answer, "'Tis new to thee" (5.1.183–84). Neither response takes precedence: innocence and experience, youth and age are as consubstantial in the play as good and evil.

While Auden was writing *The Sea and the Mirror,* he composed and made available to a seminar he was teaching at Swarthmore an extraordinarily detailed chart of a constellation of dualities in human life and thought. The chart consists essentially of three columns, the "Hell of the Pure Deed" on the left, which includes the symbol of the sea, the sin of sensuality, the tragic hero and the religion of animism; and the antithetical "Hell of the Pure Word" on the right, which includes, antithetically, the symbol of the desert, the sin of pride, the demonic villain (Iago), and the religion of logical positivism. The center column, reconciling the other two, is

"This World, Dualism of Experience, Knowledge of Good and Evil," and "Existential Being," in which the sea and the desert are reconciled in the city, sensuality and pride in anxiety, the tragic hero and demonic villain in the comic or ironic hero (Don Quixote), and animism and logical positivism in faith. At the top of the chart is the paradise of Eden, followed by the Fall, and at the bottom, successively, are Purgatory, forgiveness, and the paradise of the City of God. In this progression from Eden to the City of God and in its exhaustive conspectus of human experience, the chart is a remarkable anatomy simultaneously of Auden's imaginative understanding of the world and of his Christian faith. The chart is also specifically relevant to *The Sea and the Mirror,* since many of the oppositions and reconciliations it discriminates, as well as its final focus on forgiveness, are directly reflected in the poem.

The preface to *The Sea and the Mirror,* an address by "The Stage Manager to the Critics," a lyric that Auden wrote while he was composing "For the Time Being," presents a fundamental opposition between art and religious truth, between "the world of fact we love" and the reality of death, the "silence / On the other side of the wall." The Stage Manager contrasts the circus audience, "wet with sympathy now" for the spectacle they see and the scriptural peril of "the Flesh and the Devil" represented by "the lion's mouth whose hunger / No metaphor can fill"; and he also suggests, as Shakespeare's Prospero does in his "Our revels now are ended" speech (4.1.148–58) and in the epilogue to *The Tempest,* that the illusions of art are like the illusions of human life they imitate.

In chapter 1 of the poem, in Prospero's speech to Ariel, which Auden described to Isherwood as "The Artist to his genius," Prospero presents a similarly divided view of art in a fallen world. He associates the childhood experience of "The gross insult of being a mere one among many" with the development of his magical power, "the power to enchant / That comes from disillusion," and he says that as we look into Ariel's

> calm eyes,
> With their lucid proof of apprehension and disorder,
> All we are not stares back at what we are.

In his 1954 essay on *The Tempest,* Auden questioned Prospero's treatment of others, especially Caliban, and deprecated his forgiveness of them as "more the contemptuous pardon of a man who knows that he has his enemies completely at his mercy than a heartfelt reconciliation." In *The Sea and the Mirror* he deliberately diminishes Prospero by making the natural Caliban rather than the spiritual Ariel the spokesman for art and by gracing Caliban with the sophisticated prose style of the later works of Henry James. At the same time, Auden unquestionably identified profoundly with Prospero as an artist. In his 1947 lecture on *The Tempest,* he emphasizes that the magic of art "can give people an experience, but it cannot dictate the use they make of that experience. . . . That art thus cannot transform men grieves Prospero greatly. His anger at Caliban stems from his consciousness of this failure." "You can hold the mirror up to a person," Auden states, "but you may make him worse." The same consciousness of failure, the recognition, as he wrote in 1939 in his elegy to Yeats, that "poetry makes nothing happen," underlies Auden's depiction of Prospero in *The Sea and the Mirror.*

Oppositions arising from man's fallen condition, with a particular emphasis on the lost wholeness and innocence of childhood, also animate the speeches of the other characters in *The Sea and the Mirror,* as they are revealed on the deck of the ship taking them back to Milan. Antonio says that his own intractably evil existence compels Prospero always to remain a melancholy adult and "Never become and therefore never enter / The green occluded pasture as a child." Ferdinand's lyrical sonnet to Miranda, which Auden described in his draft as "mutuality of love begets love," expresses a serious mystical quest for "another tenderness," at the same time, Auden told Isherwood, that it "describes fucking in completely abstract words," as later Caliban, the id, speaks abstractly, in a highly mannered Jamesian style, about art. Stephano, who is dominated by his body, retreats to drink in an ineffectual attempt to recover the childhood unity of body and mind. The aged Gonzalo seeks forgiveness in memories of his boyhood, and Alonso, who like Shakespeare's character is marked by penitence as well as love for his son, advises Ferdinand how to rule the civilized city by walking a tightrope between dualities. Sebastian regresses to the fantasies of infancy, where the thought is equivalent to the deed, "Where each believed all wishes wear a crown," and he is redeemed by the failure of such thinking in the adult world. Trinculo, Stephano's opposite, has too cold and dominating a mind and seeks for the warmth of the flesh, the "Green acres" of his childhood, when he "Was little Trinculo."

Auden's attraction to childhood was partly temperamental. He wrote in *A Certain World,* "I was both the youngest child and the youngest grandchild in my family. Being a fairly bright boy, I was generally the youngest in my school class. The result of this was that, until quite recently, I have always assumed that, in any gathering, I was the youngest person present." Auden had happy childhood memories both of his family and of the Pennine landscape in which he grew up— the connection between the two is represented in "In Praise of Limestone"—and he almost always saw the years before the advent of sexuality as an image of an Edenic or paradisal state.

His interest in what Caliban calls "the green kingdom" of childhood had other religious associations for him as well. He considered the verse "Suffer little children, and forbid them not, to come unto me: for of such is the kingdom of heaven" (Matt. 19.14) an answer to "those who think of the good life as something contrary to our animal nature, that the flesh is not divine"; and he also interpreted it as a statement of the human need, not only the injunction, to "love thy neighbour as thyself," since children, who "do love and trust their neighbour naturally unless their trust is betrayed," show that such love is part of our biological nature. In addition, since he believed that the stages of growing up are not discarded but accumulated, Auden was also vocationally interested in "the child, and the child-in-the-adult" because what they most enjoy in poetry "is the manipulation of language for its own sake, the sound and rhythm of words."

Miranda's luminous villanelle, which Auden labeled "integrated love" in his draft, celebrates a vision of childhood. Her villanelle presents the joining of the mirror of art and the nature it reflects, the fundamental aesthetic duality of *The Sea and the Mirror,* in a childlike apprehension of love and matrimony. Miranda revisits Antonio's reference to the Eden of childhood, but with the "green pasture" no longer "occluded," and in the final stanza she speaks of the "changing garden," in which she and Ferdinand "Are linked as children in a circle dancing." Auden returned to the idea of children dancing in

a ring of agape in a lecture at the New School in which he
quoted a passage from Lewis Carroll's *Through the Looking-
Glass* that suggests an association of the image with the music
of the spheres. The passage describes Alice dancing with
Tweedledum and Tweedledee: "She took hold of both hands
at once: the next moment they were dancing round in a ring.
This seemed quite natural (she remembered afterwards), and
she was not even surprised to hear music playing: it seemed
to come from the tree under which they were dancing, and it
was done (as well as she could make it out) by the branches
rubbing one across the other, like fiddles and fiddlesticks. . . .
'I don't know when I began it, but somehow I felt as if I had
been singing it a long long time!'"

Auden's conception of Caliban as well as of Ariel in chapter 3 is the most radical expression of Auden's religious apprehension of dualism in *The Sea and the Mirror* as well as of
his perception of the frivolousness of art. Speaking first on
behalf of the audience, Caliban asks Shakespeare whether his
definition of art as *"a mirror held up to nature"* does not indicate the *"mutual reversal of value"* between the real and the
imagined, since on *"the far side of the mirror the general will
to compose, to form at all costs a felicitous pattern becomes the*
necessary cause *of any particular effort to live or act or love
or triumph or vary, instead of being as, in so far as it emerges
at all, it is on this side, their* accidental effect?" Caliban asks
Shakespeare how he could thus *"be guilty of the incredible
unpardonable treachery"* of introducing him into his play,
"the one creature" whom the Muse *"will not under any circumstances stand,"* the child of *"the unrectored chaos,"* *"the
represented principle of* not *sympathising,* not *associating,*
not *amusing."* He protests also, *"Is it possible that, not content*

with inveigling Caliban into Ariel's kingdom, you have also let loose Ariel in Caliban's?" In the next section of the chapter, Caliban assumes his "officially natural role" to address those in the audience who wish to become writers. He describes how the writers in the audience finally master Ariel only to discover reflected in his eyes "a gibbering fist-clenched creature with which you are all too unfamiliar . . . the only subject that you have, who is not a dream amenable to magic but the all too solid flesh you must acknowledge as your own; at last you have come face to face with me, and are appalled to learn how far I am from being, in any sense, your dish." In the final section of chapter 3, Caliban tells the audience that he begins "to feel something of the serio-comic embarrassment of the dedicated dramatist, who, in representing to you your condition of estrangement from the truth, is doomed to fail the more he succeeds, for the more truthfully he paints the condition, the less clearly can he indicate the truth from which it is estranged." Caliban finally resolves this paradox by attempting to transcend it, by acknowledging "that Wholly Other Life from which we are separated by an essential emphatic gulf of which our contrived fissures of mirror and proscenium arch— we understand them at last—are feebly figurative signs."

The dualities of nature and art Caliban describes in his long prose speech, and the frivolousness he indicts, are also represented in his style, in the deliberately antithetical juxtaposition of the flesh he embodies with the abstract language he uses. Auden had played Caliban in a school play, he associated him with Falstaff, the character in Shakespeare whom he most admired, and he was particularly proud of the style of Caliban's speech in *The Sea and the Mirror,* a speech he considered a masterpiece. He wrote to Spencer,

Caliban does disturb me profoundly because he doesn't fit in; it is exactly as if one of the audience had walked onto the stage and insisted on taking part in the action. I've tried to work for this effect in a non-theatrical medium, by allowing the reader for the first two chapters not to think of the theatre (by inversion, therefore, to be witnessing a performance) and then suddenly wake him up in one (again by inversion, introducing "real life" into the imagined).

This is putting one's head straight into the critics' mouths, for most of them will spot the James pastiche, say this is a piece of virtuosity, which it is, and unseemly levity or meaningless, which it isn't.

"Caliban (the Prick), as the personification of Nature," Auden told Spencer, "has the power of individuation, but no power of conception. Ariel, on the other hand, as the personification of Spirit, has the power of conception but not of individuation: i.e. Caliban is Ariel's Oracle." "What I was looking for was, therefore," Auden continued,

(a) A freak "original" style (Caliban's contribution), (b) a style as "spiritual,'" as far removed from Nature, as possible (Ariel's contribution) and James seemed to fit the bill exactly, and not only for these reasons, but also because he is the great representative in English literature of what Shakespeare certainly was not, the "dedicated artist" to whom art is religion. You cannot imagine him saying "The best in this kind are but shadows" or of busting his old wand. In fact Ariel fooled him a little, hence a certain Calibanesque "monstrosity" about his work.

I have, as you say, a dangerous fondness for "trucs" [ways around things, poetic tricks]; I've tried to turn this to advantage by selecting a subject where it is precisely the "truc" that *is* the subject; the serious matter being the fundamental frivolity of art. I hope someone, besides yourself, will see this.

This conception of art is critical to all of Auden's later work because it enabled him to distinguish and transform his taste for camp as well as "trucs." It helps account for his attraction to Kierkegaard's distinctions of the aesthetic, the ethical, and the religious, and it reflects his own deep religious commitment. Auden also wrote Spencer, "I'm extremely pleased and surprised to find that at least one reader feels that the section written in a pastiche of James is more me than the sections written in my own style, because it is the paradox I was trying for, and am afraid hardly anyone will get." In a review in 1944, Auden said that James "was not, like Mallarmé or Yeats, an esthete, but, like Pascal, one to whom, however infinitely various its circumstances, the interest itself of human life was always the single dreadful choice it offers, with no 'second chance,' of either salvation or damnation."

Shakespeare's representation of dualism in *The Tempest* is governed, I think, not by the Manichaeism Auden saw, though elements of it may be present, but by the Christian idea of *felix culpa*, the paradox of the fortunate fall, in which good is consubstantial with evil and can issue from it. At the outset of the action Prospero tells Miranda when she sees the shipwreck that there is "no harm done . . . No harm, / I have done nothing but in care of thee" (1.2.14–16). His care culminates in her betrothal but evolves through her suffering as well as his own, and he associates that suffering with the blessing as well as pain of their exile from Milan. They were driven from the city, he tells her, "By foul play . . . / But blessedly holp hither" (1.2.62–64), sighing "To th' winds, whose pity, sighing back again, / Did us but loving wrong" (1.2.150–51). The same motif is expressed by Ferdinand as he submits to Prospero's rule and to the ritual ordeal that Prospero contrives to

make him value the love of Miranda: "some kinds of base-
ness / Are nobly undergone, and most poor matters / Point to
rich ends. . . . The mistress which I serve quickens what's
dead / And makes my labours pleasures" (3.1.2–7). Gonzalo,
summing up the whole action of the play, says that everyone
has found himself, "When no man was his own" (5.1.213).

Auden hints at a comparable kind of paradox, though
more tenuously, in a number of the speeches of the supporting cast in chapter 2 of *The Sea and the Mirror*, especially Sebastian's, as well as at the end of Caliban's speech in chapter 3.
The sense of resolved, if not fortunate, suffering, however, is
most fully developed in the postscript, where Ariel sings of his
love for Caliban's mortality and of its completion of his own
spiritual being. Ariel speaks for the first time in the poem and
is echoed by the Prompter, who suggests the voice of Auden
as well as that of Prospero:

> Weep no more but pity me,
> Fleet persistent shadow cast
> By your lameness, caught at last,
> Helplessly in love with you,
> Elegance, art, fascination,
>   Fascinated by
>   Drab mortality;
> Spare me a humiliation,
>   To your faults be true:
> I can sing as you reply
>   . . . *I*

Ariel proposes a union of antitheses—"For my company be
lonely / For my health be ill: / I will sing if you will cry"—in
which he and Caliban will be joined not despite, but because
of, the differences between them.

Alonso, at the end of his speech in chapter 2, says that he is "now ready to welcome / Death, but rejoicing in a new love, / A new peace." The resonance of such a love Auden would also have found in *The Tempest.* At the close of the play, in the epilogue, Prospero pleads for the audience's charity as they themselves must pray for God's charity, and in the body of the play, in a climactic and well-known speech just before he renounces his art, he resolves to forgive his enemies. When Ariel tells him that his "affections" would "become tender" if he beheld the sufferings of the court party, Prospero answers,

> And mine shall.
> Hast thou, which art but air, a touch, a feeling
> Of their afflictions, and shall not myself,
> One of their kind, that relish all as sharply
> Passion as they, be kindlier moved than thou art?
> Though with their high wrongs I am struck to th' quick,
> Yet with my nobler reason 'gainst my fury
> Do I take part. The rarer action is
> In virtue than in vengeance.
>
> (5.1.18–28)

This speech, which is indebted in language as well as thought to Montaigne's analysis of the difficulty of forgiveness in his essay "Of Crueltie," may not be one to which Auden especially attended in *The Sea and the Mirror,* and he is likely to have found its elevation of reason to be symptomatic of the Manichaeism in *The Tempest* to which he objected; but the impulse to forgive is one that he deeply shared and that was always latent in his dualistic thinking. In his Swarthmore chart, it is the immediate prelude to Paradise. The idea of forgiveness is absent in the preface by the Stage Manager but is present in muted form in Prospero's speech in chapter 1.

Prospero, in Auden's presentation, speaks only briefly of forgiveness and can seem ungenerous in his response not only to
Caliban, but to other characters as well. Yet his irony does not
exclude sympathy. His speech is specifically an address to his
Muse, and in the draft even the hostile Antonio recognizes
(if sarcastically) that the purpose of Prospero's "conjuring" is
gracious: "it's wonderful / Really, how much you have man-
aged to do. . . . So they / Did want to better themselves after
all / All over the ship I hear them pray / As loyal subjects, to
be grateful enough, / Trying so hard to believe what you say /
About life as a dream in search of grace / And to understand
what you mean by the real."

The theme of forgiveness is explicit in the speeches of the
supporting cast in chapter 2. Stephano talks of the "need for
pardon" in his attempt to find union with his belly, to join
mind and matter, and Sebastian experiences a "proof / Of
mercy" that rejuvenates him. In his draft Auden indicated
"forgiveness" as the subject of Sebastian's sestina, and among
the six words he initially considered to end the lines in the
sestina were "give" and "get," terms he used to discriminate
agape and eros. Gonzalo, in the last stanza of his speech, says,
"There is nothing to forgive," and in the draft Auden had
added, "There is everything to bless." In chapter 3, Caliban
speaks to the young artist in the audience of "that music
which explains and pardons all" and of the need, "if possible
and as soon as possible, to forgive and forget the past." He
closes his speech by saying that in the "Wholly Other Life . . .
all our meanings are reversed and it is precisely in its negative
image of Judgement that we can positively envisage Mercy,"
a traditional Christian conception of Mercy as the fulfillment
of the Law that parallels the idea of the fortunate fall that

runs through *The Tempest.* In the postscript, finally, which includes overtones of Auden's relation with Kallman, the Prompter's "*I*" evokes not only Prospero the artist but also all the individual human beings whom Ariel and Caliban allegorically compose and suggests a marriage of the flesh and spirit in this world, and of Auden himself with his vocation, that is animated by forgiveness and love.

Alonso, perhaps the most moving character in *The Tempest,* speaks in his final lines in *The Sea and the Mirror* not only of his being ready to welcome death but of

> having heard the solemn
> Music strike and seen the statue move
> To forgive our illusion.

The reference is to the coming to life of Hermione's statue in Shakespeare's *The Winter's Tale* (5.3), which Auden, in his lecture on the play at the New School, saw as the finest of Shakespeare's reconciliation scenes and a perfect celebration of forgiveness. Auden's late addition of the line "To forgive our illusion"—it is not in the draft—is the most expansive of the numerous Shakespearean allusions in *The Sea and the Mirror,* comprehending the poem's deepest religious impulses as well as its deepest inspiration in Shakespeare, radiating both inward to the illusion it creates and outward to the illusion it imitates, a luminous counterpart of Prospero's grave and beautiful plea for our applause in the epilogue to *The Tempest,* a distillation of the reconciliation of agape and art that Auden sought in the poem and in his life.

CHAPTER THREE

Auden's Criticism

Auden gave many lectures and wrote an enormous number of reviews, essays, and introductions to books by other authors. *The Dyer's Hand,* his most important critical work, is composed of pieces he had previously delivered or published. He followed no critical school whatsoever, and the occasional character of his criticism was deliberate. In his brief preface to *The Dyer's Hand,* he wrote, "A poem must be a closed system, but there is something, in my opinion, lifeless, even false, about systematic criticism"; and he told Alan Ansen that he did not write out his lectures on Shakespeare at the New School in New York in 1946–47 because "criticism is live conversation." Much of the power of Auden's critical writing, and of the pleasure it gives, is due to its embodiment of these beliefs.

At the same time, Auden's criticism is deeply informed by his faith and is often an explicit testament to it. He wrote

Stephen Spender that the subject of *The Dyer's Hand* was
Christianity and art: "That is what the *whole* book is really
about, the theme which dictated my selection of pieces and
their order." (William Empson astutely identified, and expressed his offense at, precisely this theme in his review of
the book in the *New Statesman.*) The same religious purpose
animates almost all of Auden's prose works after 1940 and can
be seen clearly in the representative examples that follow: in
his treatment of the spiritual failure of classical literature and
culture; the insufficiency of romantic love; the spiritual mo-
mentousness of Shakespeare's depiction of ordinary human
existence; and the parabolic natures of *Don Quixote* and
Moby-Dick, works which he paired in *The Enchafèd Flood.*

Classical Literature and Culture

Auden interpreted classical writers teleologically, ar-
guing that classical thought was made intelligible, and its
weaknesses diagnosed and eventually resolved, by the advent
of Christianity. He was especially prompted to this view by
Charles Cochrane's *Christianity and Classical Culture*, though
he found some analogous ideas in Kierkegaard. He said that
Cochrane's book showed that whereas the culture of late antiquity had reached an impasse, an intellectual and spiritual
failure of nerve that made society incapable of coping with its
situation, the Christian faith that was crystallized by Saint Augustine evolved a religious pattern that enabled men to understand what was happening to them and to make sense of their
personal experience. As opposed to classical ideas of cosmology and history, Auden said in his review of Cochrane's book,
Augustine asserts that "there is nothing intrinsically evil in

matter" and that "history is not an unfortunate failure of necessity to master chance, but a dialectic of human choice."
Classical doctrine conceives of man "as an immortal divine
reason incarcerated in a finite mortal body"; Augustine asserts "the Christian doctrines of Man as created in the image
of God, and Man as a fallen creature." The contrast, Auden insists, making the Pauline distinction he repeated over and over
again, "is not between body and mind, but between flesh,
i.e., all man's physical and mental faculties as they exist in his
enslaved self-loving state, and spirit, which witnesses within
him to all that his existence was, and still is meant to be."
Lastly, Auden says, Augustine replaces the classical apothe-
osis of the Man-God with the Christian belief in Christ, the
God-Man, who chooses the suffering of self-sacrifice rather
than the heroism of great deeds: "The idea of a sacrificial victim is not new; but that it should be the victim who chooses
to be sacrificed, and the sacrificers who deny that any sacrifice has been made, is very new." Auden concludes by praising the consequent development of a Christian community,
but he nonetheless condemns, in the twentieth century as
well as the fourth, the political exploitation of Christianity,
the "hopes of using Christianity as a spiritual benzedrine for
the earthly city."

Recent scholarship on the early Christian era has revealed
significant oversimplifications in Cochrane's theses, which
Auden shared, particularly in his depiction of classical idealism as a static postulation of coeternal principles of mind and
matter, with no allowance for change or process, and in his
sometimes narrow view of classical politics and political philosophy. Two decades later, Auden modified his judgment of
both Cochrane and late antiquity through his reading, among

other works, of the poems of the twentieth-century Greek
writer, C. P. Cavafy, for a collection of whose poems in English translation he wrote an introduction in 1961, and of
E. R. Dodds's book *Pagan and Christian in the Age of Anxiety*, which he reviewed in 1965. Dodds was a good friend of
Auden, to whose poem *The Age of Anxiety* he alludes in the
title to his own book. Dodds states in his book, "As an agnostic I cannot share the standpoint of those who see the triumph of Christianity as the divine event to which the whole
creation moved," but "equally I cannot see it as the blotting
out of the sunshine of Hellenism"; and these perspectives enabled him to show the relation of Pagan and Christian in the
Hellenic world less tendentiously than Cochrane. While acknowledging Dodds's learning, Auden responded by saying,
"As an Episcopalian, I do not believe that Christianity did triumph or has triumphed," so that "while I consider the fourth-
century victory of Christian doctrine over Neoplatonism,
Manichaeism, Gnosticism, Mithraism, etc., to have been what
school history books used to call 'a good thing,' I consider the
adoption of Christianity as the official state religion, backed
by the coercive powers of the State . . . to have been a 'bad,'
that is to say, an un-Christian thing." Auden adds that Irenaeus, whom he says Dodds surprisingly neglects in his study,
is "my favorite theologian of the period." Irenaeus would
have been congenial to Auden because he wrote against the
Gnostics, but Auden also characteristically praises him "because, gentle soul that he was, he disliked persecution, even
of cranks."

Some of Dodds's observations, as well as Cochrane's, are
repeated in an essay entitled "The Fall of Rome" that Auden
was asked to write for *Life* magazine in 1966 (which the mag-

azine failed to publish), but he continues to insist on the rev-
olutionary significance of Christianity for art and history.
"One may like or dislike Christianity," he says in the essay,
"but no one can deny that it was Christianity and the Bible
which raised Western literature from the dead." Auden then
essentially rehearses the effects of the Incarnation on art that
he had itemized a quarter of a century earlier in Simeon's
meditation in "For the Time Being," saying that "a faith which
held that the Son of God was born in a manger, associated
himself with persons of humble station in an unimportant
Province, and died a slave's death, yet did this to redeem all
men, rich and poor, freemen and slaves, citizens and barbar-
ians, required a completely new way of looking at human beings." "If all are children of God, and equally capable of salvation," Auden says, "then all, irrespective of status or talent,
vice or virtue, merit the serious attention of the poet, the nov-
elist and the historian."

Auden's distinction between pagan and Christian literature, and the assumptions about human life that they reflect,
was categorical. He always remained conscious of classical
culture's toleration of "many evils, like slavery and the expo-
sure of infants, which should not be tolerated" and were tolerated "not because it did not know that they were evil, but
because it did not believe that the gods were necessarily
good." He also deplored the Greek tendency to compare government with art. "A society which really was like a poem,"
he wrote, "and embodied all the esthetic values of beauty,
order, economy, subordination of detail to the whole effect,
would be a nightmare of horror, based on selective breeding,
extermination of the physically or mentally unfit, absolute
obedience to its Director, and a large slave class kept out of

sight in cellars." But at the same time Auden believed that judged "by the degree of diversity attained and the degree of unity retained . . . it is hardly too much to say that the Athenians of the fifth century B.C. were the most civilized people who have so far existed"; and like cultured Englishmen of his generation, he was steeped in the classics and writes about them with a depth of familiarity and insight. He is always aware, from a Christian perspective, of what they lack, but except in the case of Plato that consciousness is used as a means of appreciating their works rather than of invidiously judging them. His eloquent treatment of the world of Homer is a good example. "The assumption of the *Iliad,*" he writes, "as of all early epics, which is so strange to us, is that war is the normal condition of mankind and peace an accidental breathing space. In the foreground are men locked in battle, killing or being killed, farther off their wives, children, and servants waiting anxiously for the outcome, overhead, watching the spectacle with interest and at times interfering, the gods who know neither sorrow nor death, and around them all, indifferent and unchanging, the natural world of sky and sea and earth. That is how things are; that is how they always have been and always will be." "The world of Homer," Auden continues, "is unbearably sad because it never transcends the immediate moment; one is happy, one is unhappy, one wins, one loses, finally one dies. That is all. Joy and suffering are simply what one feels at the moment; they have no meaning beyond that; they pass away as they came; they point in no direction; they change nothing. It is a tragic world but a world without guilt for its tragic flaw is not a flaw in human nature, still less a flaw in an individual character, but a flaw in the nature of existence."

Auden sees the same differences between Greek tragic drama and Elizabethan and modern tragedy. The tragedy of Agamemnon, Orestes, Oedipus, or Antigone, he writes, is that whatever they do must be wrong. "As in Homer, we find ourselves in a world which is quite alien to us. We are so habituated to the belief that a man's actions are a mixed product of his own free choices for which he is responsible and circumstances for which he is not that we cannot understand a world in which a situation by itself makes a man guilty." "The original sin of the Greek tragic hero is hybris," Auden explains, "believing that one is god-like. . . . The original sin of the modern tragic hero is pride, the refusal to accept the limitations and weaknesses which he knows he has, the determination to *become* the god he is not." The determination to become a god, of course, is the sin of Adam and Eve and, before them, of Satan, and in an essay on *Moby- Dick*, Auden makes clear that by the terms "modern tragedy" and "pride" he means "Christian tragedy" and the "Christian sin of Pride," though he is careful to explain, as he did repeatedly, that "in using the term Christian" he is "not trying to suggest that Melville or Shakespeare or any other author necessarily believed the Christian dogmas, but that their conception of man's nature is, historically, derived from them."

In "The Globe," an essay in *The Dyer's Hand,* Auden elaborates a number of further differences between ancient and modern drama. Time in Greek drama, he points out, is simply the time it takes for the hero's situation to be revealed, whereas in Elizabethan drama "time is what the hero creates with what he does and suffers, the medium in which he realizes his potential character." The possibility of choice, too, is different in the two dramas. "In Greek tragedy everything

that could have been otherwise has already happened before
the play begins," but in an Elizabethan tragedy, in *Othello,* for
example, there is no point before Othello actually murders
Desdemona when it would have been impossible for him to
discover the truth, "and convert the tragedy into a comedy."
Finally, Auden writes that in Greek drama the tragic heroes
either commit crimes unwittingly, like the parricide and in-
cest of Oedipus, or directly at the command of a God, like
Orestes, and they accept suffering and misfortune as "mysteriously just," since these are signs that the gods are displeased.
"But in Shakespeare," Auden says, "suffering and misfortune
are not in themselves proof of Divine displeasure. It is true
that they would not occur if man had not fallen into sin, but,
precisely because he has, suffering is an inescapable element
in life—there is no man who does not suffer—to be accepted,
not as just in itself, as a penalty proportionate to the particular sins of the sufferer, but as an occasion for grace or as a process of purgation."

There is a consequent difficulty for the modern dramatist, Auden notes. If the hero is innocent and noble and suffers great misfortune, the effect will be pathetic, not tragic.
But if the hero by his sins brings his suffering upon himself,
his character is diminished, since "there is no such thing as a
noble sinner, for to sin is precisely to become ignoble." Shakespeare and Racine, Auden argues, resolve this deficiency by
giving the sinner "noble poetry to speak, but both of them
must have known in their heart of hearts that this was a conjuring trick." Some of the "count your blessings" disposition
that provoked Hannah Arendt is at work in this view. Auden
always saw suffering as a condition of existence and was perhaps really more sympathetic to the tragic heroes of Greek

drama, who were not as directly responsible as Elizabethan tragic heroes for their suffering and were less prone to justify themselves. He did not see self-conscious and self-centered passions of great suffering the way Shakespeare clearly did, as themselves sources of detailed theatrical, as well as psychological and spiritual, interest. In another essay in *The Dyer's Hand*, he argued that the suffering depicted in literature must be "typical of the human condition" and went so far as to say that "a suffering, a weakness, which cannot be expressed as an aphorism should not be mentioned." Auden, significantly, gravitated toward an aphoristic style in his own prose and wrote a great many haiku.

Romantic Love

Auden treats romantic love irreverently throughout his work. In *A Certain World* he writes, "No notion of our Western culture has been more responsible for more human misery and more bad poetry than the supposition . . . that a certain mystical experience called falling or being 'in love' is one which every normal man and woman can expect to have." "As a result," he says, "thousands and thousands of unfortunate young persons have persuaded themselves that they were 'in love' when their real feelings could be more accurately described in much cruder terms, while others, more honest, knowing that they have never been 'in love,' have tormented themselves with the thought that there must be something wrong with them." Auden also states that he finds "the personal love poems of Dante, Shakespeare, Donne, for all their verbal felicities, embarrassing. I find the romantic vocabulary only tolerable in allegorical poems where the 'Lady' is not a real human being." He adds that "simple, or elaborate, praise of physical beauty is always charming, but when it comes to writing about the emotional relation between the sexes, whether in verse or prose, I prefer the comic or the coarse note to the hot-and-bothered or the whining-pathetic."

Auden's view of romantic love, however, is not only an expression of his personal temperament, but also reflects the religious treatment of the subject that he found in Denis de Rougemont's *Love in the Western World,* a book he reviewed in 1941 and greatly admired. A history of the romantic myth from its inception in courtly love in twelfth-century Provence down to its modern personal and political forms, de Rougemont's work essentially argued, as Auden explains in his review, that "at the root of the romantic conception of ideal sexual passion lies Manicheism, a dualistic heresy introduced into Europe from the East, which held matter to be the creation of the Evil One and therefore incapable of salvation." From this dualistic heresy, Auden says, summarizing de Rougemont, it follows that "all human institutions like marriage are corrupt, and perfection can be reached only by death, in which the limitations of matter are finally transcended. . . . The primary expression of this myth is the Tristan legend which culminates in Wagner's opera." The "negative mirror image" of the Tristan story, Auden continues, is "the legend that begins with Jean de Meung and culminates in Mozart's Don Giovanni. Here it is the flesh that is asserted and the spirit that is denied; the present moment is all, the eternal future nothing." These two "isotopes of Eros," as he called them, fascinated Auden, and he was to cite them for the rest of his life. He believed that both myths are "diseases of the Christian imagination," since they are both dependant upon

Christianity's belief in the individual, in free choice, and in one's responsibility to the temporal moment.

Opposed to Eros, de Rougemont argued, stands the Christian doctrine of agape, and Auden quotes from de Rougemont's explanation of how the Incarnation allows for the radical dilation of the idea of love by the assertion not of some future or ideal life but of "'our present life now repossessed by the Spirit.'" Auden's only quarrel is with de Rougemont's suggestion that Eros is of sexual origin and that there is a dualistic division between Agape and Eros rather than a dialectical one. "For Eros," Auden says, quoting Dante's *Purgatorio* xvii, "surely, is '*amor sementa in voi d'ogni vertute, e d'ogni operazion che merta pene*' [love, the seed within yourselves of every virtue and every act that merits punishment], the basic will to self-actualization without which no creature can exist, and Agape is that Eros mutated by Grace, a conversion, not an addition." The conversion, Auden explains, invoking the traditional Christian conception of the relation between justice and mercy, the Old Testament and the New, is "the Law fulfilled, not the Law destroyed."

Finally, Auden especially praises de Rougemont's defense of the Christian doctrine of marriage, which Auden says will offend both the hedonist and the romantic. Auden always honored the state of marriage. His poetry in the early 1940s is frequently preoccupied with the sacrament of matrimony and its capacity to unite husband and wife in one flesh; and he sought out and was close friends with many married couples and their families throughout his life. He was drawn to, and often quoted, Kierkegaard's statement in *Either/Or* that "romantic love can very well be represented in the moment, but conjugal love cannot, because an ideal husband is not one who is such once in his life but one who every day is such." "If I would represent a hero who conquers kingdoms and lands," Kierkegaard continued in *Either/Or*, "it can very well be represented in the moment, but a cross-bearer who every day takes up his cross cannot be represented either in poetry or in art, because the point is that he does it every day." Kierkegaard's view is contradicted by much modern literature, notably Joyce's *Ulysses*, but Auden himself, characteristically, disparaged Joyce precisely for accepting "flux as the Thing-in-Itself" and was deeply sympathetic to Kierkegaard's position. "Like everything which is not the involuntary result of fleeting emotion but the creation of time and will," Auden wrote, "any marriage, happy or unhappy, is infinitely more interesting and significant than any romance, however passionate."

In his introduction to *The Protestant Mystics* in 1964, Auden contrasts Plato's and Dante's accounts of the vision of eros as a prefiguration of a higher love. "What is so puzzling about Plato's description" of the ladder of love in *The Symposium*, Auden says, "is that he seems unaware of what we mean by a person." In *The Symposium*, Diotima says that in order to ascend to absolute Beauty, the lover "'should begin by loving earthly things for the sake of the absolute loveliness, ascending to that as it were by degrees or steps, from the first to the second, and thence to all fair forms; and from fair forms to fair conduct, and from fair conduct to fair principles, until from fair principles he finally arrive at the ultimate principle of all, and learn what absolute Beauty is.'" Auden's response to this celebrated description is that "it is quite true, as you say, that a fair principle does not get bald and fat or run away with somebody else. On the other hand, a fair principle cannot give me a smile of welcome when I come into the room.

Love of a human being may be, as you say, a lower form of love than love for a principle, but you must admit it is a damn sight more interesting." In "No, Plato, No," a poem he wrote at the end of his life, Auden repeats this objection: "I can't imagine anything / that I would less like to be / than a disincarnate Spirit," though he says he can imagine that his Flesh, whose "ductless glands" have been "slaving twenty-four hours a day / with no show of resentment," might well want to be rid of *him:* "yes, it well could be that my Flesh / is praying for 'Him' to die, / so setting Her free to become / irresponsible Matter."

Dante, on the other hand, Auden points out, does not entertain such Platonic disjunctions. "He sees Beatrice, and a voice says, 'Now you have seen your beatitude.'" She is to him a human creature, "a 'graced' person," and his vision and memory of her as a beautiful human being remains with him to the very last moment, when he takes the step "from the personal creature who can love and be loved to the personal Creator who is Love. And in this final vision, Eros is transfigured but not annihilated." "Whatever else is asserted by the doctrine of the resurrection of the body," Auden continues, "it asserts the sacred importance of the body. As Silesius says, we have one advantage over the angels: only we can each become the bride of God. And Juliana of Norwich: 'In the self-same point that our Soul is made sensual, in the self-same point is the City of God ordained to him from without beginning.'"

Shakespeare

In his concluding lecture on Shakespeare at the New School in 1947, Auden said that one could argue for hours as to what Shakespeare believed, "but his understanding of psychology is based on Christian assumptions. . . . All men are equal not in respect of their gifts but in that everyone has a will capable of choice. Man is a tempted being, living with what he does and suffers in time, the medium in which he realizes his potential character. The indeterminacy of time means that events never happen once and for all. The good may fall, the bad may repent, and suffering can be, not a simple retribution, but a triumph." "*Un*-Christian assumptions," Auden continued, include the ideas "first, that character is determined by birth or environment, and second, that man can become free by knowledge, that he who knows the good will will it. Knowledge only increases the danger, as Elizabethans saw." "The third un-Christian assumption," Auden said, "is the understanding of God as retributive justice, where success is good and failure means wrong, and where there is no need for forgiveness or pity. In modern books, character is entirely the victim of circumstances, and there is the daydream of people as angels, transcendent in their power."

Some of the results of responding to the plays with these premises are immediately evident in Auden's lectures as well as essays on Shakespeare, some are less obvious. The tragic heroes Auden treats as essentially sinners, and the comedies, particularly the last plays, he treats as movements toward a redeemed community, as representations of the fulfillment of eros in Christian agape. Such perspectives on the plays were not uncommon in academic scholarship in the middle of the twentieth century, and they characterized T. S. Eliot's criticism of Shakespeare in its earlier decades, but the difference between the generosity and inclusiveness of Auden's Christian Shakespeare and the frequent narrowness of Eliot's, or the academy's, is immense. Auden was a friend of Eliot but never shared his religious or social prejudices. He objected emphatically to Eliot's statement in 1934 in *After Strange Gods* that the population of "the society we desire" should be "homogeneous" and have "a unity of religious background; and reasons of race and religion combine to make any large number of free-thinking Jews undesirable." With his usual prescience, Auden said of the book in a letter to Eliot, "Some of the general remarks, if you will forgive my saying so, rather shocked me, because if they are put into practice, and it seems quite likely [they will be], would produce a world in which neither I nor you I think would like to live." In a review two decades later, Auden also criticized Eliot's snobbish intimation in *The Family Reunion* and *The Cocktail Party* that intelligent, upper-class characters in the plays had the privilege of an inner Christian calling, while stupid or lower-class characters did not. Auden was free of such insularity, and his treatment of Shakespeare's plays and characters, unlike Eliot's, is animated by a spacious understanding of a great variety of men and women made momentous by their decisions in a life ultimately illuminated by the ideas of original sin and grace, a religious apprehension of ordinary human experience that gives his response to Shakespeare its originality and power.

Auden's stunning lecture at the New School on *Antony and Cleopatra,* his favorite Shakespearian play, is a clear example. Auden frequently spoke of characters in literature as if they were "people," and, where he could, he tried to understand authors themselves in the same way. It is a distinguishing characteristic of his criticism. In his lectures and essays on Shakespeare, he thus freely imagines and talks of Shakespeare's characters as people whom one "might meet and have dinner with and talk to" rather than as purely fictional constructions, and he treats Antony and Cleopatra as such dinner companions. In the process he demystifies the play without diminishing it. Academic criticism of *Antony and Cleopatra* at the time Auden spoke and in the half century following spends itself in disputes over whether the play depicts love or lust or both, whether its ending is transcendental, whether its numerous oxymorons and oscillating movements ever come to rest, whether the imaginative splendor of its poetry is in conflict with the reality of its action. Auden cuts through these tangles by understanding the play's shimmering complexity in its presentation of "worldliness." He remarks that the "physical attraction" between Antony and Cleopatra "is real, but both are getting on, and their lust is less a physical need than a way of forgetting time and death." "When Romeo and Juliet express their love," he remarks, "they are saying, 'How wonderful to feel like this.' Benedick and Beatrice talk as they do about love to test each other. Antony and Cleopatra are saying, 'I want to live forever.' Their poetry, like fine cooking, is a technique to keep up the excitement of living." The flaws in the great tragic heroes, Auden continues, constitute particular and "pure states of being," but "Antony and Cleopatra's flaw . . . is general and common to all of us all of the time: *worldliness*—the love of pleasure, success, art, ourselves, and conversely, the fear of boredom, failure, being ridiculous, being on the wrong side, dying. If Antony and Cleopatra have a more tragic fate than we do, that is because they are far more successful than we are, not because they are essentially different." At the conclusion of the lecture, Auden asks, "Why is the weather so good in *Antony and Cleopatra?* In other plays nature reflects vices or hostility, but it is important in *Antony and Cleopatra* that the world be made to seem infinitely desirable and precious. The whole world of the play is bathed in brilliant light. In the last plays, physical tempests stand for suffering through which people are redeemed. The tragedy in *Antony and Cleopatra* is the refusal of suffering." "The splendor of the poetry," Auden says, "expresses the splendor of the world in this play, and the word 'world' is constantly repeated. 'Com'st thou smiling from / The world's great snare uncaught?' (IV.viii.17–18), Cleopatra asks. But Antony is caught. What Caesar calls Cleopatra's 'strong toil of grace' (V.ii.351) is the world itself and in one way or another it catches us all."

These passages are, I think, fundamentally right about *Antony and Cleopatra,* and they show the simultaneous focus and inclusiveness of Auden's religious treatment of the play. Auden's interpretation is incisively, even severely, moral, without being moralistic. He sees the worldliness of *Antony and Cleopatra* in traditional Christian terms, but those terms enlarge as well as crystallize the play. They are not merely homiletic, and they are certainly not dismissive. Like Shakespeare, he is entirely open to the glories of the world at the same time that he is uncompromising about them. The political as well as erotic life of these legendary pagan figures clearly fascinated Shakespeare and gave rise to some of his most resplendent poetry, but Shakespeare's mind was also, as Auden would say, on agape, and he was never for a moment distracted from Antony and Cleopatra's ordinary humanity and frailty. It is that ordinariness—"the love of pleasure, success, art, ourselves, and conversely, the fear of boredom, failure, being ridiculous, being on the wrong side, dying"—as much as their quite remarkable rhetoric, that makes their portraiture so fertile and compelling. Indeed, Shakespeare's genius in the play, which Auden apprehends perspicuously, is to make their extraordinary poetry a function of their ordinary mortality.

Auden also sees Christian charity in Shakespeare's depiction of Falstaff in the *Henry IV* plays. Characteristically, Auden not only responds to Falstaff as he would to a living person, but also claims that he doesn't really belong in the play. He writes in his essay "The Prince's Dog," "At a performance, my immediate reaction is to wonder what Falstaff is doing in this play at all. . . . for the better we come to know Falstaff, the clearer it becomes that the world of historical reality which a Chronicle Play claims to imitate is not a world which he can inhabit." Hal, later Henry V, Auden sees as a particularly unsympathetic example of that reality. In his lecture on the play in 1946, he says, "Prince Hal. Yes, he is the Machiavellian character, master of himself and the situation —except that in the last analysis Falstaff is right when he tells him, 'Thou art essentially mad without seeming so.'" "Hal has no self," Auden continues. "He can be a continuous success because he can understand any situation, he can control himself, and he has physical and mental charm. But he is cold as a fish. . . . Hal is the type who becomes a college president, a government head, etc., and one hates their guts."

Falstaff Auden conceives of as Hal's antitype. In his lecture he asks, "Why do people get fat?—because they eat humble pie as their food and swallow their pride as their drink. What does drink do? It destroys the sense of time and makes one childlike and able to return to the innocence one enjoyed before one had sex." Auden usually treated "childlikeness" as a spiritual state of innocence, and in his rich and

subtle essay on the *Henry IV* plays he elaborates the implications of that association by interpreting Falstaff, with his
"gross paunch and red face," as at once a reminder of the sickness in England's body politic and as a parabolic image of a
love that is not of this world: "Overtly Falstaff is a Lord of
Misrule; parabolically, he is a comic symbol for the supernatural order of Charity as contrasted with the temporal
order of Justice symbolized by Henry of Monmouth." "From
the point of view of society," Auden writes, Falstaff's way of
choosing his conscripts

> is unjust, but if the villagers who are subject to conscription
> were to be asked, as private individuals, whether they would
> rather be treated justly or as Falstaff treats them, there is no
> doubt as to their answer. . . . Falstaff's neglect of the public
> interest in favor of private concerns is an image for the jus-
> tice of charity which treats each person, not as a cipher, but
> as a unique person. The Prince may justly complain:
>
> > I never did see such pitiful rascals
>
> but Falstaff's retort speaks for all the insulted and injured
> of this world:
>
> Tut tut—good enough to toss, food for powder, food for
> powder. They'll fit a pit as well as better. Tush, man, mortal
> men, mortal men.

"Falstaff never really does anything," Auden notes, "but he
never stops talking, so that the impression he makes on the audience is not of idleness but of infinite energy. He is never
tired, never bored, and until he is rejected he radiates happiness as Hal radiates power, and this happiness without apparent cause, this untiring devotion to making others laugh becomes a comic image for a love which is absolutely self-giving."

Auden's discussion of Falstaff's evocation of Christian charity can seem like a willful fantasy—Empson, for example, found it outrageous. But Falstaff does, as Auden sees, lie athwart these plays and radically call Hal's world into question. There is no critic who can avoid having to try to explain (away) the calculating inhumaneness of Hal's view of Falstaff in his opening soliloquy or who can deny the peculiar penetration of Falstaff's remark, "food for powder." Both passages in fact troubled Empson, and he had to rely on his conception of the double plot finally to accommodate them. But, as Auden I think sees correctly, the two plots really are of a different order, certainly aesthetically, and Falstaff's character, if not a transparent parable of charity, does nonetheless give intimations of the childlike freedom and comic plenitude of another and better world. "Food for powder" is hardly a Christian homily, but perhaps the full weight of its criticism is made possible only by a society in which each person is enjoined to love his neighbor as himself. After Auden finished his lecture on *Henry IV* and *Henry V* at the New School, Alan Ansen, who was a student in the class, asked him if he really thought Shakespeare would have approved of his interpretation. Auden answered, "I don't care whether he would or not. It's in the text, and that's what counts. . . . And it is Falstaff who is really remembered." It is, and arguably no one has remembered him better than Auden.

A similar religious focus distinguishes Auden's lectures and essays on *Othello* and *The Merchant of Venice.* For a variety of reasons, including his temperamental aversion to the idea of romantic love, he is uninterested in Othello or his suffering, and he badly misconstrues the idealism, indeed Scriptural idealism, of Desdemona's love for Othello, a love that may be said, by his own definition, to be "absolutely self-giving." He dismisses Desdemona as simply "a young school-girl who wants above all to be a grown-up." He repeats the charge in his essay "The Joker in the Pack." But Auden's essentially religious apprehension of Iago, a character with whom his own sense of being an outsider had affinities, is profound. In his lecture he treats Iago as an incarnation of Saint Augustine's conception of the *acte gratuit* that is represented in the episode in the *Confessions* in which Augustine describes his theft, as an adolescent, of pears from an orchard, explaining that he stole them for no other reason than the doing of it, the doing of it, as Auden says, "just for the hell of it," solely to assert his will. Auden also relates Iago to the idea of an inverted saint, a saint *manqué* ("I am not what I am" [1.1.65], Iago says, in a direct parody of Scripture) as well as to the conception of man's perversity presented in Dostoevski's *Notes from Underground,* man's need to prove that "men are still men and not the keys of a piano, which the laws of nature threaten to control so completely that soon one will be able to desire nothing but by the calendar. . . . the whole work of man really seems to consist in proving to himself every minute that he is a man and not a piano-key!" In his essay on the play Auden has a less ostensible religious focus, and he considers how the nature of Iago's character is expressed and functions in modern society as well as in the Venetian society of the play, thus viewing him not only as a Machiavellian villain, but also as a self-destructive practical joker, "a parabolic figure for the autonomous pursuit of scientific knowledge through experiment which we all, whether we are scientists or not, take for granted as natural and right." He also compares Iago to a psychiatrist: "Iago treats Othello

as an analyst treats a patient except that, of course, his intention is to kill not to cure. Everything he says is designed to
bring to Othello's consciousness what he has already guessed
is there." In both the essay and the lecture Auden is actually
imagining, as Shakespeare does, and with corresponding bril-
liance, what the Devil would be like if he were made flesh and
dwelt among us.

A simultaneously religious and social sensibility is also
deeply at work in Auden's treatment of Shylock's confrontation with society in *The Merchant of Venice*. In his essay
"Brothers & Others," he examines medieval and Renaissance
conceptions of usury to show how "spiritual usury" is made a
metaphor of Christian faith in the play, and he also insists that
money is an inescapable medium of exchange in "a world in
which, irrespective of our cultural traditions and our religious
and political convictions, we are all mutually dependent. This
demands that we accept all other human beings on earth as
brothers, not only in law, but also in our hearts." Auden shows
his typical cosmopolitan receptiveness to other cultures and
religions in this statement, but its sentiment is nonetheless
clearly Christian. In his lecture on *The Merchant of Venice*,
in some respects more revealing than his elegantly argued
essay, Auden discusses Shylock primarily as a social outsider
and relates him to the "frivolous" Gentile society of the play:
"Whenever a society is exclusive, it needs something ex-
cluded and unaesthetic to define it, like Shylock. The only serious possession of men is not their gifts but what they all possess equally, independent of fortune, namely their will, in
other words their love, and the only serious matter is what they
love—themselves, or God and their neighbor." "The people in
The Merchant of Venice are generous," Auden continues,

"and they behave well out of a sense of social superiority. Outside of them is Shylock, but inside is melancholy and a lack of
serious responsibilities—which they'd have as farmers or
producers, but not as speculators. They are haunted by an
anxiety that it is not good sense for them to show." "I am glad
that Shakespeare made Shylock a Jew," Auden says. "What is
the source of anti-Semitism? The Jew represents seriousness
to the Gentile, which is resented, because we wish to be frivolous and do not want to be reminded that something serious
exists. By their existence—and this is as it should be—Jews
remind us of this seriousness, which is why we desire their
annihilation." Auden had made a similar distinction several
years earlier, in the midst of World War II, in his "Lecture
Notes" in *The Commonweal:* "Modern anti-Semitism . . . is
one symptom of a Christendom which has taken offense at
faith, but finding that nothing means social breakdown, is determined to replace it by a pagan political religion." "The Jew
is persecuted," Auden wrote, "because he cannot deceive
himself. His witness is this—either faith or nothing. Whereas
a corrupt Christendom wants to say: 'Faith is too difficult;
nothing is despair; we must have no God but Caesar. There
might be no harm, though, in Caesar being a cleric.'"

There is possibly no more liberating a way of talking about
the theology of *The Merchant of Venice* than by contrasting
the frivolous Christian and the serious Jew. The contrast is
not reductive; Auden is dispassionately open to different sides
of the confrontation; and he clearly appreciates the tone and
pleasures of the frivolous society he calls to judgment. It is
entirely characteristic that he should talk in the lecture about
how "hard cases make bad law" and compare Portia to a "shys-
ter lawyer" at the same time he points out that Shylock finally

"alienate[s] our sympathy, even though we can understand his wanting revenge," not because he is a Jew, but at least in part "because he tries to play it safe and use the law, which is universal, to exact a particular, personal revenge. A private quest for revenge may have started a feud, but would be forgivable. What is not forgivable is that he tried to get revenge safely." Auden's analysis discriminates *The Merchant of Venice*'s religious ideas without submerging the play in theological discourse, and it remains fully alive to its theatrical intricacy and poise. His resulting fidelity to the extraordinary mixture of social textures and tones in the confrontation of Christian and Jew in the play is a function of his imaginative intelligence, but it stems as well from the generosity and "seriousness" of his own faith.

A religious view of the world also deeply informs Auden's criticism of *King Lear*. In his discussion of the play in "Balaam and the Ass" (1954), later reprinted in *The Dyer's Hand*, he focuses on the Fool and treats his character at once as a representation of Lear's sense of reality (hence his disappearance once Lear goes mad) and, like all Renaissance fools, as intermittently "the voice of God using him as His mouthpiece." In his earlier, more comprehensive lecture on *King Lear* at the New School in 1947, Auden says of its many repetitions of the word "nature" that "the real counterpointing in the play is the world of passion, of *man's* nature, versus the elements, the physical world of the universe." In his lecture on *Troilus and Cressida*, interestingly, Auden says that in the Homeric world as well "human emotion is juxtaposed against the indifference of everlasting nature," but he explains the juxtaposition of the two in the nominally pagan cosmos of *King Lear* by invoking Pascal's contrast of man and the infinite in *Pensées*.

He also compares *King Lear* to opera: "The quality common to all the great operatic roles is that each of them is a passionate and willful state of being, and in recompense for the lack of psychological complexity, the composer presents the immediate and simultaneous relation of these states to each other." "The crowning glory of opera," he continues, "is the big ensemble. The Fool, Edgar, and the mad Lear compose such a big scene in *King Lear.* The ensemble gives a picture of human nature, though the individual is sacrificed." Auden interprets the whole of the play in a similar way: "This is a profoundly unsuperstitious play. I do not agree that it is a nihilistic or pessimistic one. Certain states of being—reconciliation, forgiveness, devotion—are states of blessedness, and they exist while other people—conventionally successful people— are in states of misery and chaos." The meaning of the excruciating suffering in *King Lear* has been debated by critics for centuries, but Auden's inclusive and strikingly unsentimental view of it may be the most wise. It has affinities with his luminous religious depiction in "Musée des Beaux Arts" of "the human position" of suffering in everyday life.

Cervantes and Herman Melville

In an essay on Christianity and art, Auden wrote, "There can no more be a 'Christian' art than there can be a Christian science or a Christian diet. There can only be a Christian spirit in which an artist, a scientist, works or does not work. A painting of the Crucifixion is not necessarily more Christian in spirit than a still life, and may very well be less." He added that "the only kind of literature which has gospel authority is the parable, and parables are secular stories with

no overt religious reference." Auden was particularly drawn
to the genre of parable, and his understanding of it underlies
much of his literary criticism. He discriminated various degrees of parable and treated Kafka, for example, as "a great,
perhaps the greatest, master of the pure parable," remarking
that whereas sometimes in real life we can meet a man and
think he comes straight out of Shakespeare or Dickens, "nobody ever met a Kafka character." On the other hand, whereas
we could never describe an experience of our own as Dick-
ensian or Shakespearian, we can have what we recognize as
Kafkaesque experiences. Auden interpreted the English detective story, which he discusses in "The Guilty Vicarage," as a
slightly more mixed genre, still largely parabolic, but one which
depicts some characters, the detectives Sherlock Holmes and
Father Brown, for example, with whom one can at least begin
to identify. "In the detective story," Auden writes, "as in its
mirror image, the Quest for the Grail, maps (the ritual of
space) and timetables (the ritual of time) are desirable. Nature should reflect its human inhabitants, i.e., it should be the
Great Good Place; for the more Eden-like it is, the greater the
contradiction of murder." "The detective story addict," Auden
says, indulges "the fantasy of being restored to the Garden of
Eden, to a state of innocence, where he may know love as love
and not as the law." Auden, finally, treats Dickens's *Pickwick
Papers* as a novel with fully concrete characters, situations,
and actions that flourish for their own sake but are at the
same time illuminated by a parabolic meaning. Auden says
that "the real theme of *Pickwick Papers*—I am not saying that
Dickens was consciously aware of it—and, indeed, I am
pretty certain he was not—is the Fall of Man. It is the story
of a man who is innocent, that is to say, who has not eaten of

the Tree of the Knowledge of Good and Evil, and is, therefore, living in Eden." "He then," Auden continues, "eats of the Tree, that is to say, he becomes conscious of the reality of Evil but, instead of falling from innocence into sin—this is what makes him a mythical character—he changes from an innocent child into an innocent adult who no longer lives in an imaginary Eden of his own but in the real and fallen world."

Don Quixote and *Moby-Dick* Auden treats essentially as he does *Pickwick Papers,* not as pure parables, but as mythopoeic secular stores of parabolic religious significance. In *The Enchafèd Flood,* a series of lectures he gave at the University of Virginia that were published in 1950, Auden contrasted Cervantes and Melville at length, interpreting Don Quixote as an ironically mad hero in a comic universe, and Ahab as a tragically mad hero in a tragic universe. Auden defines a hero in the lectures as an exceptional individual "who possesses authority over the average," and, drawing upon Kierkegaard, he discriminates three kinds of heroic authority: the aesthetic, the ethical, and the religious. Kierkegaard's (and Auden's) distinctions among the three are numerous, but essentially the aesthetic hero is one to whom fortune has given exceptional gifts either of talent or situation; the ethical hero—Socrates is an example—is one who at any given moment is related to universal truth of which he happens to know more than others, a knowledge that is not confined to "what is commonly called ethics"; and the religious hero is "one who is committed to anything with absolute passion, i.e., to him it is the absolute truth, his god." "The distinction between being absolutely committed to the real truth, and being absolutely committed to falsehood," Auden says, "is not between being a religious man or not being one, but between the sane and the mad."

"Don Quixote," Auden argues, "is, of course, a representation, the greatest in literature, of the Religious Hero." Not a knight, but only the poor, plain Alonso Quixano, Don Quixote reads about knight errantry in romances and becomes slightly mad when he sells land to buy books of romance. He suddenly goes really mad as he sets out to imitate the heroes of the romances he admires. "Naturally enough," Auden observes, "he fails in everything. When he thinks he is attacking giants, heretics and heathens he is not only worsted in combat, but attacks innocent people and destroys other people's property." Auden notes particularly that even "when his vision is sane, i.e., when he sees that the windmills are windmills and not giants, it does not change his original conviction, for he takes his moments of sane vision to be mad and says, 'These cursed magicians delude me, first drawing me into dangerous adventures by the appearances of things as they really are and then presently changing the face of things as they please.'"

In other essays, Auden sees Don Quixote as specifically a Christian hero, an ironic portrait of a Christian saint. Auden distinguishes between a tragic madness like Macbeth's and the madness of Don Quixote, who lacks arete, who fails but is never discouraged, and who himself suffers intentionally while making others suffer only unintentionally. Auden also distinguishes between madness and faith, offering a definition of faith that he repeats in numerous works: "To have faith in something or someone means a) that the latter is not manifest. If it becomes manifest, then faith is no longer required. b) the relation of faith between subject and object is unique in every case. Hundreds may believe, but each has to believe by himself." "Don Quixote," Auden says, "exemplifies both.

a) He never sees things that aren't there (delusion) but sees them differently, e.g., windmills as giants, sheep as armies, puppets as Moors, etc. b) He is the only individual who sees them thus."

Don Quixote's faith is not idolatrous, Auden continues, because he "never expects things to look after him; on the contrary he is always making himself responsible for things and people who have no need of him and regard him as an impertinent old meddler." But he never loses faith and despairs. His friends, Auden says, consider the Romances he loves historically untrue and stylistically naive. "Don Quixote, on the other hand, without knowing it, by his very failure to imitate his heroes exactly, at once reveals that the Knight-Errant of the Romances is half-pagan, and becomes himself the true Christian Knight." Auden remarks that in the inn, when Don Quixote imagines the hunchback maid is the daughter of the Governor of the Castle, who has fallen in love with him and is trying to seduce him, "the language is the language of Eros, the romantic idolisation of the fair woman, but its real meaning is the Christian agape, which loves all equally irrespective of their merit."

The saintliness of Don Quixote's character, Auden maintains, is enriched by his relation to Sancho Panza: "Don Quixote's lack of illusions about his own powers is a sign that his madness is not worldly but holy, a forsaking of the world, but without Sancho Panza it would not be Christian. For his madness to be Christian, he must have a neighbor, someone other than himself about whom he has no delusions but loves as himself." Sancho Panza, in turn, Auden considers a "'holy' realist," who follows his master out of love and who celebrates everyday human existence, "who enjoys the actual and immediate for its own sake, not for any material satisfaction it provides"—which for Auden was itself an article of Christian faith.

Finally, Auden writes, "however many further adventures one may care to invent for Don Quixote—and, as in all cases of a true myth, they are potentially infinite—the conclusion can only be the one which Cervantes gives, namely that he recovers his senses and dies." He must say to his friends, "'Ne'er look for birds of this year in the nests of the last: I was mad but I am now in my senses: I was once Don Quixote de la Mancha but am now the plain Alonso Quixano, and I hope the sincerity of my words and my repentance may restore me to the same esteem you have had for me before.'" "In the last analysis," Auden says,

> the saint cannot be presented aesthetically. The ironic vision gives us a Don Quixote who is innocent of every sin but one; and that one sin he can put off only by ceasing to exist as a character in a book, for all such characters are condemned to it, namely, the sin of being at all times and under all circumstances interesting.
> Analogy is not identity.
> Art is not enough.

Auden's interpretation of Don Quixote resembles his treatment of Falstaff—he conceives of both of them as essentially childlike—and is open to some of the same objections: it is hyperbolic as well as parabolic, and its awareness of the ironies in the depiction of Don Quixote's character, especially the suffering his foolishness inadvertently causes others, is perhaps also deliberately circumscribed. On the other hand, Auden richly discriminates the childlike innocence of the picaresque fantasy world of the novel, and his view of Don

Quixote as an unconsciously holy fool, rather than diminishing or falsifying his character, enlarges it. Agape may not be an inapposite term to describe the mythic dimension of both Don Quixote and Falstaff, one doleful, the other endlessly witty, and it may also be the best explanation of why they are as cherished by their readers and audiences as they seem to have been by their authors.

Melville's Ahab Auden treats as Don Quixote's antitype, a religious hero who is demonic in a tragic universe, where Don Quixote is saintly in a comic one. The whole of *Moby-Dick*, he argues, is "an elaborate synecdoche" in which whale fishing becomes an image of all men's lives and is full of parable and typology, including the characters and names of the nine ships. The white whale, however, is an example of a symbol "in the real sense." "A symbol is felt to be such," Auden says, "before any possible meaning is consciously recognised; i.e. an object or event which is felt to be more important than the reason can immediately explain is symbolic." "Secondly," Auden continues, "a symbolic correspondence is never one to one but always multiple, and different persons perceive different meanings." Ahab, who is defined by such symbolic thinking, declares, "All visible objects, man, are but pasteboard masks." "To me," he says, "the white whale is that wall shoved near to me. Sometimes I see there's naught beyond. I see in him outrageous strength with an insatiable malice sinewing it. That inscrutable thing is chiefly what I hate." The extremity of Ahab's hatred Auden relates to Kierkegaard's definition of defiant, as opposed to weak, despair in *Sickness unto Death*. "With hatred for existence," Kierkegaard says, defiant despair "wills to be itself, to be itself in terms of its misery; it does not even in defiance or defiantly will to be itself, but to be itself in spite." The defiant despairer "will not hear about what comfort eternity has for him . . . because this comfort would be the destruction of him as an objection against the whole of existence." "Of this despair," Auden comments, "Ahab is a representation, perhaps the greatest in literature."

Ahab's earlier loss of his leg to Moby-Dick and his subsequent accident, causing a wound, Melville says, that "all but pierced his groin," would come at the end of a Greek tragedy, a punishment of the gods for hybris, Auden comments, but in Melville they come at the beginning, so that we watch what kind of individual Ahab *becomes*, exceptional because of "'*being* what others are not,'" not "'*becoming* what one wills or God wills for one.'" Auden particularly notes his reaction "when he breaks his leg, jumping off the *Enderby*, whose captain has lost an arm to Moby-Dick without despairing and whose doctor ascribes Moby-Dick's apparent malice to clumsiness." "The example of sanity with authority is too much for Ahab," Auden says, "and he must again goad himself to his resolution," vowing, "I now prophesy that I will dismember my dismemberer. Now then, be this prophet and the fulfiller one. That's more than ye, ye great gods, ever were."

We watch Ahab "enact every ritual of the dedicated Don Quixote life of the Religious Hero, only for negative reasons," Auden observes. He throws away his pipe, not as an ascetic renunciation, but to prevent distraction from the task he has set himself. He sets up the Doubloon as a reward for the first person to sight Moby-Dick, though he has no intention of letting anyone but himself be the first, and at the same time, violating every spiritual condition of an oath, he coercively makes the harpooneers swear to pursue Moby-Dick to the

death. Later, he baptizes his harpoon, "a perversion of the
Knight Errant's act of dedicating his arms," and he throws
away the ship's quadrant, cursing science as a "vain toy" that
casts "man's eyes aloft to the heavens," a "defiant inversion in
pride," Auden remarks, "of the humility which resists the
pride of reason, the theologian's temptation to think that
knowledge of God is more important than obeying Him."
"Next," Auden says, he places the child Pip in his place in the
captain's cabin and takes the humble position of the lookout,
"an inversion of 'He who would be greatest among you, let
him be as the least.'" "Lastly," Auden remarks, in refusing to
help his neighbor, the captain of the *Rachel*, who asks for help
in finding his young son, Ahab "counterfeits the text: 'If any
man come to me and hate not his father and mother and wife
and children and brethren and sisters, yea and his own life
also, he cannot be my disciple.'"

Auden's analysis of Ahab, as of *Moby-Dick* as a whole, is
exceptionally responsive to Melville's peculiar amalgamation
of metaphysical apprehension and concrete psychological and
natural detail. It is tempting in interpreting Melville to make
a one-to-one allegory of the former or to become immersed
in the particulars of the latter. Auden does neither, and though
in seeking to make *Moby-Dick* entirely intelligible in Christian terms he may to some extent ignore the reasons that led
Melville in a letter to Nathaniel Hawthorne in November
1851 to call his novel a "wicked book," he may also reveal its
essential Christian foundation more clearly. Hawthorne wrote,
after a long visit by Melville in 1856, that Melville could "neither believe, nor be comfortable in his unbelief; and he is too
honest and courageous not to try to do one or the other."
Auden was obviously less troubled by that combination and

may therefore have seen the matrix of Melville's religious sensibility more clearly.

The Enchafèd Flood presents a similarly subtle religious and parabolic analysis of *Billy Budd,* but Auden's more simplified treatment of the novella and its author in his early poem "Herman Melville" perhaps reveals the plumb line of his Christian interests even more clearly. The poem was written in 1939 and though less ambitious than his later, more famous elegies, it deserves to be ranked among them for its critical as well as imaginative power. In the first stanza, Auden describes Melville in his later years, after he had completed the "nightmare" of *Moby-Dick:*

> Towards the end he sailed into an extraordinary mildness,
> And anchored in his home and reached his wife
> And rode within the harbour of her hand,
> And went across each morning to an office
> As though his occupation were another island.

Auden depicts *Billy Budd* as a product of this mildness, as a work that anchored Melville's continued metaphysical speculation to dining tables and drawing rooms, to ordinary human existence:

> Evil is unspectacular and always human,
> And shares our bed and eats at our own table,
> And we are introduced to Goodness every day,
> Even in drawing-rooms among a crowd of faults;
> He has a name like Billy and is almost perfect,
> But wears a stammer like a decoration:
> And every time they meet the same thing happens;
> It is the Evil that is helpless like a lover
> And has to pick a quarrel and succeeds,
> And both are openly destroyed before our eyes.

At the end of the poem, Auden returns to Melville the man and, with a luminous quotation from Melville's letter of November 1851 to Hawthorne, he depicts the vision of the Eucharist and agape that incorporated Melville in the hallowed daily life of the community:

> Reborn, he cried in exultation and surrender
> "The Godhead is broken like bread. We are the pieces."

> And sat down at his desk and wrote a story.

CHAPTER FOUR

"Horae Canonicae"

As Ursula Niebuhr observed, Auden's Christianity was far too exploratory and capacious to be pigeonholed. He can be said to have veered between the Anglican and Roman Churches during much of his lifetime, but in significant respects his religious thinking always comprehended both. He told Golo Mann that "in each of us, there is a bit of a Catholic and a bit of a Protestant; for truth is catholic, but the search for it is protestant," and he consistently saw the relation between the catholic truth and the protestant search dialectically. As he said, analogously and repeatedly, "the Way" rests upon faith and skepticism, "faith" that the divine law exists and that our knowledge of it can improve, and "skepticism" that our knowledge of these laws can ever be perfect.

Auden was extremely interested around the time of his conversion in the writings of Karl Barth, Paul Tillich, and Reinhold Niebuhr, the radical mid-twentieth-century Protestants who rediscovered Kierkegaard. Auden read translations of Kierkegaard himself intently in the 1940s and greatly admired his existential views of religious experience, though he came to quarrel sharply with Kierkegaard's failure to recognize man's bodily existence. He agreed with Barth's view of the limitations of human reason and culture in the face of the transcendent Word, though he questioned the consequent "Barthian exaggeration of God's transcendence which all too easily becomes an excuse for complacency about one's sins and about the misfortunes of others." In his note to a line in "New Year Letter" that mentions "Reason's depravity," Auden quoted, with implicit approval, Tillich's statement in *The Interpretation of History* that "the fundamental Protestant attitude is to stand in nature, taking upon oneself the inevitable reality; not to flee from it, either into the world of ideal forms or into the related world of super-nature, but to make decisions in concrete reality." Tillich, in addition, stressed that the human relation to the divine must be private and subjective, a view to which Auden also emphatically subscribed. As he said in discussing Don Quixote, "The relation of faith between subject and object is unique in every case. Hundreds may believe, but each has to believe by himself." Auden was attracted to Niebuhr's religious thought as well. He especially valued Niebuhr for his Augustinian interpretation of the power of sin in this world, man's refusal "to admit his 'creatureliness,'" his attempt "to be more than he is," his inescapable temptation, individually as well as in the social and political organizations he forms, perpetually to succumb to the sin of pride. At the same time, he praised Niebuhr for not retreating from this world either to Stoic apathy or to Platonic dualism and its idealization of reason. Niebuhr's conception of the place of faith in this fallen world, like Tillich's, led him to ceaseless political and social activism. Auden's disillusionment as a quasi-political spokesman in the 1930s, as well as his increasing aversion to the presumption of artists, made him wary of active political engagement, but his sense of the need to rectify social and political injustice was equally acute, if less optimistic.

The most important strain of thought Auden derived from all these writers, I think, one that encouraged his own deepest instincts, was that faith must be understood in the reality of the here and now. He did not believe that human existence should be conceived as a preparation for an afterlife, and he reacted with distaste to the notion that one would be compensated for suffering in this world by reward in the next. As he wrote to Clement Greenberg and repeated in various ways in other contexts, "Eternity is the decision *now,* action now, one's neighbour *here.*"

The insistence on this spiritual understanding of the here and now, as well as on the subjective uniqueness of each individual's faith, is especially apparent in Auden's treatment of sacred history. In his manuscript notes for the television broadcast of parts of "For the Time Being" in 1967, he wrote that "any religion which regards certain historical events, the bringing of Israel out of Egypt, for example, or the birth of Christ, as sacred and redemptive, unique revelations of the nature of God, presents the faithful with certain complications. On the one hand the event lies in the historical past and cannot be repeated. On the other hand, the believer has at every moment to renew his faith in its personal significance for him in his present time and place." "In our age and society," he continued, "an author can no longer assume, as his ancestors could, that his audience is, at least officially, Christian. He has there-

fore to try to write something which will have meaning for
others as human beings, whether they are believers or unbelievers." In "For the Time Being," he added, "I tried to
hold the balance between past and present, without demand-
ing that the audience share my convictions. Whether I have
succeeded or failed, is for others to judge." I think the judgment must be that he did succeed, if not entirely in "For the
Time Being" itself, then certainly in many of his other poems,
including "Horae Canonicae," which is a consummate representation at once of sacred history and twentieth-century experience. There is indeed an underlying balance between
past and present throughout Auden's work, which helps explain its extraordinary reach. The balance both sustains and is
sustained by his profound religious convictions, but, as he
suggests, it affects his readers and audiences first of all as
human beings.

Auden not only conceived of particular events of biblical
history in concrete contemporary terms but also imagined
how he himself would have responded to those events had he
been there. This was especially true of his conception of the
meaning of the Crucifixion. He viewed the Crucifixion as fundamentally a reenactment of the Fall by postlapsarian men
and women, and he judged people, including himself, by how
they would have behaved if they had been onlookers. It was
an imaginative habit that is related to his wish to have "conversations" with dead authors as well as with characters in
their works. In his draft notes on religion and theology, he
wrote, in a passage repeated with slight variations in *A Certain World,* "As we were all in Adam, so were we all in Jerusalem on that first Good Friday when there was as yet no Easter,
no Pentecost, no Christians. Who was I, I ask myself, and what

was I doing? One of the disciples, in a state of spiritual despair and physical terror? Ridiculous. . . . One of the Sanhedrin? No. I am not *that* a devout churchman. Pilate? I am no political big-wheel." "No," Auden continues, "I see myself as a Hellenised Jew from Alexandria taking an afternoon stroll with a friend, engaged in a philosophical argument. Our path takes us near Golgotha. I look up and see a familiar sight, three crosses surrounded by a crowd of onlookers. 'Really,' I say, 'it's disgusting the way the mob enjoy such things. Why can't they execute criminals quickly and mercifully by giving them, like Socrates, a draft of hemlock?'" "Then," Auden writes, "I banish the disagreeable spectacle from my mind, and we resume our fascinating discussion about the nature of the True, the Good, and the Beautiful." It is this kind of imaginative interest that informs "Horae Canonicae."

The seven poems that make up "Horae Canonicae" correspond to the canonical hours, the divine offices of the church, the set times for prayer and meditation every three hours of the day. The normal sequence of the offices is Prime (6:00 a.m.), Terce or Tierce (9:00 a.m.), Sext (noon), Nones (3:00 p.m.), Vespers (6:00 p.m.), Compline (9:00 p.m.), Matins (midnight), and Lauds (3:00 a.m.). Terce, Sext, and Nones are the offices normally associated directly with the Passion, but Auden relates all of the poems in "Horae Canonicae" to the Crucifixion. He omits Matins and treats Lauds as a celebration of the dawning of the day after the Crucifixion, a day of renewal and worship. He began thinking of the poems in 1947 and wrote them from 1949 to 1954.

The canonical hours, or offices, originated in the devotional practices of the ascetic desert monks and were eventually absorbed into the worship of the public church in the

fourth century. The offices were less affected by the Refor-
mation than the liturgy itself and have remained essentially
similar in both Roman Catholic and Protestant churches. As
Dom Gregory Dix explains, the life of the church was significantly enlarged by the incorporation of the personal, self-
edifying worship of the monks into public worship: "The
monk and his imitators gave the church the divine office and
the conception of the *whole* life of man as consummated in
worship, instead of regarding worship as a department of life,
like paganism, or the contradiction of daily life, like the pre-
Nicene Church." In "Horae Canonicae" Auden responds profoundly not only to this fundamental conception of the daily
life of a Christian but also to the largest consciousness of his
own whole life as consummated in worship. The sanctified
progression of time Auden records in the poem is in the first
instance a devotional representation of the changes in his own
body and mind, with a particular focus on the body, in the
course of a day, but it exfoliates into a representation of the
natural cycle of human life and the course of secular and divine history.

In a lecture at Swarthmore College in March 1950, in
which he discussed "Prime" to illustrate the process of writing a poem, Auden said he became interested in the offices
because they celebrate historical events, "particularly events
of the Passion of Christ," and that what he had in mind in
"Horae Canonicae" was a series of poems "about the relation
of history and nature," a problem that he said had fascinated
him for at least a decade. He defined natural events as members of classes of similar events that are related by the principle of identity and that occur necessarily and rhythmically,
according to "laws-*of*," the kind of laws discovered by science,

the law of gravity, for example. A historical event, on the other hand, which is a product of human will, is "unique . . . a member of a class of one"; it does not occur necessarily according to law, but voluntarily (though it may be judged by man-made laws, "laws-*for*"); and it "is the cause of subsequent historical events, in the sense that it provides them with a motive for occurring." Historical time is unilinear and its events are related by the principle of analogy. Of a natural event "it *could* only be said that it is what it is," of an historical event, "that it *could* have been otherwise."

Both the poet and the historian, Auden noted, are concerned with history, the events for which human beings are individually or collectively responsible, but a poet, unlike a historian, must also be concerned with the natural world in which men and women live and to which they are necessarily related. Auden's consistent interest in the natural world stemmed from two of his deepest beliefs: that "everything that is is holy," as he said in *The Prolific and the Devourer*, and that because of the Incarnation, matter, the natural order, is not a Platonic illusion or the cause of evil, but real and redeemable. He said as well, in an introduction to a volume in the Yale Series of Younger Poets, that however difficult the apprehension of Nature may be in an age of technology, "so long as we have bodies, however we may maltreat them, our relation to her has not been severed." He was particularly interested in natural landscapes and their psychological and spiritual associations, including limestone uplands like those in which he grew up as a boy, igneous rocks, volcanoes, and a precipitous and indented seacoast. He included all of these in his personal picture of Eden, and they appear in a large number of his poems. He was also continually interested in the natural life of animals, whom he celebrated as creatures exempt from the self-divisive consequences of man's fall. Surrounding all of these interests was also Auden's prophetic environmental consciousness. He believed unreservedly in the holiness of the ecology of the entire planet and was deeply disturbed by the increasing despoliation of the earth by twentieth-century technology.

Underlying Auden's distinctions between nature and history was his fundamental and abiding absorption with the duality of the many and the one, of human beings as natural, biological creatures, not unlike animals, and human beings as unique self-conscious individuals, who are responsible for their own moral choices. He touches on the subject briefly in his Swarthmore lecture as well as in "Nature, History and Poetry" in 1950, an essay which is largely a transcription of the lecture, but he develops it in more detail in "The Things Which Are Caesar's," another essay written in the same year. He notes in this essay that the creation of man is described in Genesis as "a double act." "First, 'The Lord God formed man of the dust of the ground.' Man, that is to say, is a natural creature subject like all other creatures to the laws of the natural order. Secondly, 'The Lord God breathed into his nostrils the breath of life; and man became a living soul.' Man, that is, is also a unique creature made in the image of God with self-consciousness and free will, capable, therefore, of making history." God's creation of the two sexes "and thus of human relationships," Auden continues, is also described as twofold in Genesis. God's command "Be fruitful and multiply" discriminates man as a natural creature, one who "is related impersonally to others by natural needs which are not his but function through him to maintain life and perpetuate the species"; and His declaration that "it is not good that man be alone" defines man as a unique individual who desires and is capable of entering into unique relations with others.

Later in his life, in his sermon at Westminster Abbey, Auden elaborated his comments on the account of the creation in Genesis. He said that although we are all members of the human species, all of us also possess a "'second nature,'" which we have acquired through the society and culture in which we live. For unlike members of other species, whose evolutions are complete, "every human individual is . . . endowed with a unique personal consciousness which is a trinity-in-unity—as St Augustine says, I am knowing and willing; I know that I am and will; I will to be and to know—able to answer I in response to the thous of other persons, and through his own choices to create a history for which he is accountable." He added that "the myth of our common descent from a single ancestor, Adam, is a way of expressing the fact that, as persons, we are called into being, not by any biological process, but by other persons: each of us, in fact, *is* Adam, an incarnation of all mankind."

All of these beliefs and distinctions are brought to bear on Auden's representation of the Crucifixion in "Horae Canonicae" as at once the defining historical event of Christianity and a continuing parable of faith. Auden wrote that if a man who professes to be a Christian is asked why he believes in Jesus, he can give no more objective an answer than that "'I believe . . . because He is in every respect the opposite of what He would be if I could have made Him in my own image." "Thus," says Auden, "if a Christian is asked: 'Why Jesus and not Socrates or Buddha or Confucius or Mahomet?' perhaps all he can say is: 'None of the others arouse *all* sides of my being to cry 'Crucify Him.'"

"Prime"

In his lecture at Swarthmore, Auden explained, with regard specifically to "Prime," that he had always been interested in "the experience of waking up," the "problem of return to consciousness and the return of memory and identity, the whole relation of the ego and self." The relation of the ego and self and the quest for wholeness were subjects that Auden treated ceaselessly and intricately in essays and lectures, often, as in his lecture on Shakespeare's *Richard III*, with frustrating opaqueness. In the Swarthmore lecture, however, he talks relatively clearly of "the self-consciousness of man" as consisting of, first, the "consciousness of the self as self-contained, as embracing all of which it is aware in a unity of experiencing"; second, as "the consciousness of 'beyondness,' of the ego standing as a spectator over against both itself and the external world"; and third, as "the ego's consciousness of itself as a striving toward, of desiring to transform the self it owns, to realize its potentialities."

In the lecture at Swarthmore Auden said also that in addition to the psychological problem of waking up, there was a general theological problem which had interested him for some time, namely, "to what extent we have any kind of recollection, or imagination, or intuition of what life was like before the fall." "Since the fall is a condition of human history," he said, "as in the mythical way in which it is formulated, it seems to me we cannot imagine an unfallen action, but only the state preceding action, and action, of course, includes not only the physical action, but the actual intention of the will. And that, you see, began to link up the business of waking up." The linkage of psychology and theology was always im-

portant to Auden's thinking (as he said in 1929, "The point of psychology is to prove the Gospel"), and by the time he wrote "Horae Canonicae" the two had become virtually inseparable in his mind, each dilating, defining, and supporting the meaning of the other. This entwinement of his quite complicated sense of himself and his faith is especially apparent in "Prime."

Auden explores the emergence of the body as well as the mind from sleep in the poem. In the first stanza he is particularly interested in the sense, prior to becoming fully awake, of a self that is not yet subject to division, whose body and mind are still of a piece, a unity he associates with prelapsarian innocence. The "kind / Gates of the body fly open," but the "gates of the mind" both "swing to" and "swing shut" in order to "Quell the nocturnal rummage / Of its rebellious fronde," the dreams of night that have been "Disenfranchised, widowed and orphaned" by the "historical mistake" of Adam's Fall. The wars of the Fronde in seventeenth-century France, as Auden explained in the lecture, appeared to him to be a good image for "a rebellion against centralization of the self," which seemed to him what happens during a dream. After leaving this rebellious rummage of the night, the self can begin to awaken: "Without a name or history I wake / Between my body and the day."

The second stanza celebrates this fleeting Edenic state: "Holy this moment, wholly in the right," and the pun on holy and feeling whole is of course significant for Auden. "The world is present, about," the stanza continues,

> And I know that I am, here, not alone
> But with a world and rejoice
> Unvexed, for the will has still to claim
> This adjacent arm as my own,

> The memory to name me, resume
>   Its routine of praise and blame,
> And smiling to me is this instant while
>   Still the day is intact, and I
> The Adam sinless in our beginning,
>   Adam still previous to any act.

Not being alone, but with the world and rejoicing unvexed: these were Auden's own quests.

The third and final stanza of the poem examines Auden's full return to consciousness and his repossession of his will, the will corrupted by the fall:

> I draw breath; that is of course to wish
>   No matter what, to be wise,
> To be different, to die and the cost,
>   No matter how, is Paradise
> Lost of course and myself owing a death.

The wish "to be wise, / To be different" is the wish to be autonomous and alludes to the eating of the fruit of the tree of good and evil and the consequent loss of Eden, the subject of Milton's epic *Paradise Lost.* "Myself owing a death" indicates the condition of mortality brought about by the Fall and in addition alludes to Hal's cry to Falstaff before the battle of Shrewsbury in Shakespeare's *Henry IV, Part One,* "Why, thou owest God a death" (V.i.127), which is a reference to the common medieval and Renaissance understanding of life as a loan that must be repaid with spiritual interest.

The poem, which focuses on Christ's death in Jerusalem, then turns to the mid-twentieth-century Italian landscape (and its English associations) in which Auden wrote "Prime" and concludes with Auden fully awake and conscious, his

> ready flesh
> No honest equal, but my accomplice now,
> My assassin to be, and my name
> Stands for my historical share of care
> For a lying self-made city,
> Afraid of our living task, the dying
> Which the coming day will ask.

The flesh, now no longer an "honest equal" to the spirit, has Auden's usual Pauline signification of both the fallen mind and fallen body; the historical share is Auden's participation in the creation of a civilized city that is not of God; and the dying that the coming day will ask is, of course, the murder of Christ. The poem in its entirety, like those succeeding it in "Horae Canonicae," is an image of Auden's assimilation of his faith, of the world of nature, and of both secular and Christian history into his own sense of being.

"Terce"

"Terce" is an ironic, almost sardonic, representation of ordinary human beings preparing in the morning for the ordinary life of a day which is not going to be ordinary. The opening lines, "After shaking paws with his dog / (Whose bark would tell the world that he is always kind), / The hangman sets off briskly over the heath," place the coming crucifixion in the context of the animal kingdom, which Auden depicts later in the sequence as well, in "Nones" and "Lauds." The dog's "kind" bark is both of his kind, an unvexed, uncorrupted expression of his whole constitution that is not possible for fallen human beings, and kind in its friendliness. The hangman, judge, and even the poet "taking a breather," who "Does

not know whose Truth he will tell," are, like all of us, still idol-
aters, each in "his secret cult" praying "to an image of his
image of himself":

> "Let me get through this coming day
> Without a dressing down from a superior,
>   Being worsted in a repartee,
> Or behaving like an ass in front of the girls."

The final stanza begins:

> At this hour we all might be anyone,
> It is only our victim who is without a wish,
>   Who knows already (that is what
> We can never forgive. If he knows the answers,
>   Then why are we here, why is there even dust?).

Auden here alludes to the problem of free will and God's
foreknowledge, but also to the spiritual gap between Christ
and perishable humanity which His sacrifice will help bridge.
Christ, the victim,

> Knows already that, in fact, our prayers are heard,
>   That not one of us will slip up,
> That the machinery of our world will function
>   Without a hitch . . .
>   knows that by sundown
> We shall have had a good Friday.

The ironic tone of the entire poem is distilled in the pun on
having had "a good Friday" and is enriched by Auden's faithful attention to what Kierkegaard called the merely "aesthetic"
human wishes and "machinery of the world," an attention
which Auden habitually insisted was itself made possible for a
poet by the Incarnation.

"Sext"

"Sext," noon, the hour the Passion began, is again an ironic poem, one whose mixture of tones is more subtle than that of "Terce" because Auden sees virtue as well as corruption in the subjects he treats. Part 1 of the poem focuses on vocation, a topic that always interested him:

> You need not see what someone is doing
> to know if it is his vocation,
>
> you have only to watch his eyes:
> a cook mixing a sauce, a surgeon
>
> making a primary incision,
> a clerk completing a bill of lading,
>
> wear the same rapt expression
> forgetting themselves in a function.

The forgetting of the self "in a function" was usually an experience Auden praised and often considered in religious terms. In his review of Violet Clifton's life of her husband in 1932, for example, he had equated such intensity of attention with love. In "Sext," however, intensity of attention is animated by something quite different. The poem argues that the "eye-on-the-object look" was the result of the transfer of man's worship from the appetitive goddesses like Aphrodite and Demeter to patron saints like Saint Barbara, and that there should be monuments and odes to those who first forgot themselves in a function, "the first flaker of flints," for example, "who forgot his dinner." "But for them," we should be

Feral still, unhousetrained . . .

slaves of Dame Kind, lacking
all notion of a city,

and, at this noon, for this death,
there would be no agents.

The "flaker of flints," however, led to equivocal vocations, and
Saint Barbara became the patron saint of artillery makers.
Not to be a slave of nature, to have a "notion of a city," to be
a free "agent" are all human enfranchisements, but Christ was
also killed by them.

The irony continues, more caustically, in part 2 of "Sext,"
in which Auden examines authority and the power necessary
to exert it. Watch the mouth of a "besieging general" when he
sees "a city wall breached by his troops," of a bacteriologist realizing why his hypothesis was wrong, or a prosecutor who
"from a glance at the jury . . . knows that the defendant will
hang." Their expressions are

not of simple pleasure at getting
their own sweet way but of satisfaction

at being right, an incarnation
Of *Fortitudo, Justicia, Nous.*

You may not like them much,
(who does?) but we owe them

basilicas, divas,
dictionaries, pastoral verse,

the courtesies of the city:
without these judicial mouths

(which belong for the most part
to very great scoundrels)

> how squalid existence would be
> tethered for life to some hut village . . .

> and, at this noon, there would be no authority
> to command this death.

In part 3, the final section of "Sext," Auden turns to "the crowd" that passively watches the Crucifixion, that worships the "Prince of this world," the Devil, and that lacks any redeeming virtue. In his lectures, articles, and reviews, Auden repeatedly distinguished a crowd from a society and a community. He defined a community in a late work as a group of individuals united "by a love of something other than themselves, God, music, stamp-collecting or what-have-you." In the Swarthmore lecture in which he discusses "Prime," he said that a society is "a system that loves itself." The members of a society are united by the functioning of the whole, as in a string quartet, where the members must play their parts, but need not individually love music. The crowd, however, "loves neither itself nor anything other than itself." Its members are united only by "togetherness."

In "Sext,"

> the crowd stands perfectly still,
> its eyes (which seem one) and its mouths

> (which seem infinitely many)
> expressionless, perfectly blank.

The crowd allows no individual vision. Individuals may wonder "how many will be burned alive" in battle, the crowd does not wonder:

> The crowd sees only one thing
> (which only the crowd can see),

> an epiphany of that
> which does whatever is done.

The individual believes in God in a unique way—no two ways
are exactly the same—but for the members of the crowd
"there is only one way of believing." "Few people accept each
other . . . but the crowd rejects no one," and

> Only because of that can we say
> all men are our brothers,
>
> superior, because of that,
> to the social exoskeletons: When
>
> have they ever ignored their queens,
> for one second stopped work
>
> on their provincial cities, to worship
> The Prince of this world like us,
>
> at this noon, on this hill,
> in the occasion of this dying?

The "togetherness" that is the reason all men are brothers
is a travesty of loving one's neighbor as oneself and is of
course highly ironic, as is every other detail in these stanzas:
men's vaunted superiority to the "social exoskeletons," the
ants and bees, because they admit everyone indiscriminately
to the crowd; the worship of the Prince of this world rather
than God; the dying—the murder—that is the crowd's
epiphany.

In his review of Dodds's *Pagan and Christian in the
Age of Anxiety* in 1966, Auden wrote, "When the New Testament speaks of the 'The Prince of this world,' it certainly
does not mean the Prince of the Cosmos nor assert that, so

long as they are on earth, human souls have no option but to obey the orders of the Devil. By *this world* is meant, I should guess, Leviathan, the Social Beast." Auden elaborates the idea of "Leviathan, the Social Beast," another name for the crowd, in several poems in which he refers to Thomas Hobbes, the seventeenth-century philosopher and author of *Leviathan*. In "City Without Walls," he writes of "factories in which the functional / Hobbesian man is mass-produced"; in "Talking to Myself," he notes that "for human congregations . . . as Hobbes perceived, / the apposite sign is some ungainly monster"; and in "Address to the Beasts," he simply disparages Hobbes as one of the "clever nasties." Auden also said in his review of Dodds that "one may or may not hold the Devil responsible, but, when one considers the behavior of large organized social groups throughout human history, this much is certain; it has been characterized neither by love nor by logic." Writing during the Cold War, Auden treated the lack of love and logic as an apocalyptic peril.

The concept of "the Social Beast" may also have had further theological overtones for Auden. In his introduction to Anne Fremantle's *The Protestant Mystics* he seems to relate it, if indirectly, to the idea of original sin. "When we speak of being 'born in sin,' of inheriting the original sin of Adam," he writes, "this cannot mean, it seems to me—I speak as a fool—that sin is physically present in our flesh and our genes. . . . From the moment consciousness first wakes in a baby (and this may possibly be before birth) it finds itself in the company of sinners, and its consciousness is affected by a contagion against which there is no prophylaxis."

"Nones"

"Nones" incorporates the themes and interests of all the poems in "Horae Canonicae," but it focuses most on the consequences of the corrupt human will for the earth as well as for humankind. What is "revealed to a child in some chance rhyme / Like *will* and *kill* comes to pass / Before we realize it," the poem begins:

> It is barely three,
>   Mid-afternoon, yet the blood
> Of our sacrifice is already
>   Dry on the grass.

In Milton's *Paradise Lost* (IX, 782–84), when Eve ate the apple,

> Earth felt the wound, and nature from her seat
> Sighing through all her works gave signs of woe
> That all was lost.

Auden recapitulates that wound in "Nones," but the woe he anticipates is the actual undoing of the earth. The crowd on the hill has dispersed, he says:

> The faceless many who always
> Collect when any world is to be wrecked,
>   Blown up, burnt down, cracked open,
> Felled, sawn in two, hacked through, torn apart.

The Madonnas with the green woodpecker, the fig tree, the yellow dam, "Turn their kind faces from us"—of their kind and kindly, like the dog's kind bark in "Terce"—holy faces that are the images of our duty to nature and God; and after the deed normal human occupations and pleasures are emptied: "wherever / The sun shines, brooks run, books are written, / There will also be this death." The murder may be misrepresented, excused, denied, mythified, but "Sooner than we would choose / Bread will melt, water will burn, / And the great quell begin." "Our great quell" is what Lady Macbeth calls the murder of Duncan (I.vii.72) that plunges Scotland into a Hell that torments men and nature alike. The meltdown and scorching of the earth is the twentieth century's nuclear equivalent.

In the final stanza of the poem, Auden writes of the renewal of the body after the deed, restoring "the rhythm / We spoil out of spite," an allusion to the idea of man's perverse need to assert himself that Auden called the *acte gratuit*. In "Nones" the rhythm begins to be restored as valves close and open properly, glands secrete, vessels expand and contract, and "essential fluids / Flow to renew exhausted cells." The body and its organs do not know "quite what has happened," but are

> awed
> By death like all creatures
> Now watching this spot, like the hawk looking down
> Without blinking, the smug hens
> Passing close by in their pecking order,
> The bug whose view is balked by grass,
> Or the deer who shyly from afar
> Peer through chinks in the forest.

In *Macbeth*, after the "great quell," nature reacts in sympathy with the murder: owls are reported to have killed falcons and horses to have eaten each other. In "Nones," nature, if not entirely indifferent, is independent, a spectator to man's suffering, which is how Auden interpreted Shakespeare's portrayal of nature in *King Lear.* Animals are dispassionately present at the Crucifixion in "Musée des Beaux Arts" as well, as "dogs go on with their doggy life and the torturer's horse / Scratches its innocent behind on a tree." Though the animals are indifferent to the Crucifixion in "Musée des Beaux Arts" and not awed by it as they are in "Nones," in both poems the animal bystanders are innocent of the murder and offer nature's contrast and reproach to the guilt of civilized human beings.

Auden greatly admired D. H. Lawrence's poems on animals and plants, saying that in them Lawrence's usual anger and frustration with human beings "vanish, *agape* takes their place, and the joy of vision is equal to the joy in writing." Auden himself often praises animals, plants, and landscapes for their unself-conscious harmony. He writes in "The Maze" in 1940,

> Anthropos apteros, perplexed
> To know which turning to take next,
> Looked up and wished he were a bird
> To whom such doubts must seem absurd.

In "Their Lonely Betters" he says it seems "only proper that words / Should be withheld from vegetables and birds," and that neither the robin running through its "Robin-Anthem" nor the "rustling flowers" waiting for a third party "To say which pairs, if any, should get mated" are "capable of lying" or of assuming "responsibility for time." In "Reflections in a Forest," he writes that

> trees are trees, an elm or oak
> Already both outside and in,
> And cannot, therefore, counsel folk
> Who have their unity to win.

In "Bird-Language," he writes that the words that birds utter can betoken fear as well as rage, bravado, and lust, but that "All other notes that birds employ / Sound like synonyms for joy." In "In Due Season," finally, Auden notes that "flowers think . . . concretely in scent-colors"

> and beasts, the same
> Age all over, pursue dumb horizontal lives
> On one level of conduct and so cannot be
> Secretary to man's plot to become divine.

The unity of being in animal life is the theme of two other poems that are relevant to "Nones": "The Creatures" in 1936, written before Auden's formal renewal of faith, and "Address to the Beasts" in 1973, written in the last year of his life. In "The Creatures" he refers to the "affections and indifferences" of animals and says they offer at once a glimpse of our past Edenic innocence and a prospect of our future because though their "Pride" is "hostile to our Charity, . . . what their pride has retained, we may by charity more generously recover." What the animals' pride has retained, it can be inferred, is their un-reflective unity of being—not unlike the tree Auden praises in "Reflections in a Forest"—a unity which man can recover only through "Charity," a word whose connotation in "Creatures," though it is an early poem, is inescapably Christian.

"Address to the Beasts" begins with a contrast between human and animal life. "For us who, from the moment / we first are worlded, / lapse into disarray," it is a joy to be sur-rounded on earth by animals who are harmonious, who are "adulted," their development complete, and who "promptly and ably / . . . execute Nature's policies." Animals may kill, but not as we do:

> Of course, you have to take lives
> to keep your own, but never
> kill for applause.

Animals have no need "to become literate," the poem continues, recollecting the thought of both "Their Lonely Betters" and "Bird Language":

> but your oral cultures
> have inspired our poets to pen
> dulcet verses,

> and, though unconscious of God,
> your sung Eucharists are
> more hallowed than ours.

Their "sung Eucharists," an image that superbly condenses the liturgy and nature, are more hallowed because they proceed from the wholeness of their being, for Auden almost a sign of grace. Small birds and a cock sing such songs at the end of "Horae Canonicae," in "Lauds."

"Vespers"

"Vespers" is concerned with the rebuilding of civilization after the Crucifixion. It begins by referring to a hill "overlooking our city" that "has always been known as Adam's Grave," which at dusk (the hour of Vespers) looks as if its "right arm" is "resting for ever on Eve's haunch." This description of "the scandalous pair" sets the tone for the remainder of the poem, even its more serious conclusion. The "Sun and Moon supply their conforming masks" to people, "but in this hour of civil twilight all must wear their own faces." It is the hour, Auden says, when "our two paths cross," and "Both simultaneously recognize his Anti-type: that I am an Arcadian, that he is a Utopian."

Auden discusses the Arcadian and the Utopian in a lecture on literary Edens reprinted in *The Dyer's Hand,* distinguishing the Arcadian whose dream of Eden looks backward from the materialist Utopian whose dream of New Jerusalem looks forward. The Arcadian "knows that his expulsion from Eden is an irrevocable fact and that his dream, therefore, is a wish-dream which cannot become real." The Utopian, "on the other hand, necessarily believes that his New Jerusalem is a dream which ought to be realized so that the actions by which it could be realized are a necessary element in his dream; it must include images, that is to say, not only of New Jerusalem itself but also of the Day of Judgment." For most of the poem, Auden treats the two—"I" the Arcadian and "he" the Utopian—as irreconcilable opposites:

> He would like to see me cleaning latrines: I would like to
> see him removed to some other planet.
>
> Neither speaks. What experience could we possibly share?

The poem explores the differences between them, most of them "aesthetic," in Kierkegaard's sense of the term. "In my Eden," the Arcadian says, "a person who dislikes Bellini has the good manners not to get born: In his New Jerusalem a person who dislikes work will be very sorry he was born." Auden also develops political and moral distinctions. In Eden the "only source of political news is gossip"; in New Jerusalem "there will be a special daily in simplified spelling for nonverbal types." Eden has "compulsive rituals and superstitious tabus but we have no morals"; New Jerusalem has empty temples "but all will practise the rational virtues."

The tone of the last third of the poem is more grave. Auden wrote in *The Dyer's Hand* that "while neither Eden nor New Jerusalem are places where aggression can exist, the Utopian dream permits indulgence in aggressive fantasies in a way that the Arcadian dream does not." "Even Hitler," Auden imagines, "would have defined his New Jerusalem as a world where there are no Jews, not as a world where they are being gassed by the million day after day in ovens, but he was a Utopian, so the ovens had to come in." Auden's connection of the Utopians with Hitler suggests an association of the Utopian in "Vespers" with those who have authority in "Sext," whom nobody can like, who are "for the most part . . . very great scoundrels," and who command the Crucifixion. The Arcadian in "Vespers" thus fears that when the Utopian "closes his eyes, he arrives, not in New Jerusalem, but on some august day of outrage . . . when the unrepentant thieves (including me) are sequestered and those he hates shall hate themselves instead." The "unrepentant thieves" recollects the two thieves who were crucified with Christ, and with that implicit reference, the Arcadian returns to the Cross and asks if his encounter with the Utopian is not "also a rendezvous between two accomplices, who, in spite of themselves, cannot resist meeting":

> forcing us both, for a fraction of a second, to remember our victim (but for him I could forget the blood, but for me he could forget the innocence),
>
> on whose immolation (call him Abel, Remus, whom you will, it is one Sin Offering) arcadias, utopias, our dear old bag of a democracy are alike founded:
>
> For without a cement of blood (it must be human, it must be innocent) no secular wall will safely stand.

Abel was murdered by his brother Cain, in biblical history the first murder; Remus was murdered by his twin brother Romulus, the mythical founder of Rome. The blood in "cement of blood" is finally the blood of the Eucharist, the redeeming blood of Christ, but it also suggests unremitting human bloodshed.

"Compline"

In a review of a book by the naturalist Loren Eisley in 1970, Auden wrote that as individuals we rejoice that we are biologically members of a species, "that we are not alone, that all of us, irrespective of age or sex or rank or talent, are in the same boat." As "unique persons," however, we all also resent "that an exception cannot be made in our own case. We oscillate between wishing we were unreflective animals and wishing we were disembodied spirits, for in either case we should not be problematic to ourselves." "Compline," a counterpart to "Prime," deals with falling asleep, which like awakening profoundly interested Auden because for a few brief moments our bodies and minds are in harmony. The opening lines of "Compline" celebrate the body's escape from consciousness as one begins to fall asleep:

> Now, as desire and the things desired
>   Cease to require attention,
> As, seizing its chance, the body escapes,
>   Section by section, to join
> Plants in their chaster peace which is more
>   To its real taste, now a day is its past,
> Its last deed and feeling in, should come
>   The instant of recollection
> When the whole thing makes sense.

The instant of recollection comes, but all that is recalled are

> Actions, words, that could fit any tale,
>   And I fail to see either plot
> Or meaning; I cannot remember
>   A thing between noon and three.

In the second stanza Auden speculates that "maybe / My heart is confessing her part / In what happened to us from noon till three," or that the constellations of stars "Sing of some hilarity beyond / All liking and happening." Acknowledging the inability to know what happened, he scorns "All vain fornications of fancy" and accepts the separation of the body from the world. In "For the Time Being," Simeon speaks similarly of the "promiscuous fornication with her own images" from which poetic imagination is redeemed by the Incarnation.

The subject of the third stanza is the entry into dreams, with "its unwashed tribe of wishes" that are finally

> one step to nothing,
> For the end, for me as for cities,
> Is total absence: what comes to be
> Must go back into non-being.

The last stanza of the poem is a prayer that ends with a picnic. "Can poets be saved (can men in television) / Be saved?" the stanza begins deflatingly, but the immediately following lines offer a penitential prayer:

> *libera*
> *Me, libera* C (dear C)
> And all poor s-o-b's who never
>   Do anything properly, spare
> Us in the youngest day when all are
>   Shaken awake, facts are facts,

> (And I shall know exactly what happened
> Today between noon and three).

Not unlike Auden's Christmas letter to Chester Kallman, these lines are at once a particular prayer for Kallman, "C (dear C)," and a prayer, quoting the Requiem Mass, for the souls of all human beings. The "youngest day" is both the next day, the day of renewal in which Christians remember and acknowledge their guilt, and also the last day, when they wake up to the Last Judgment.

The final four lines turn to a paradisal vision, with Auden's customary emphasis on the ecstatic movement of a communal dance, in which

> we, too, may come to the picnic
> With nothing to hide, join the dance
> As it moves in perichoresis,
> Turns about the abiding tree.

"Picnic," in addition to its sense of an informal pastoral gathering, includes the idea of eating, always potentially for Auden an image of selfishness transformed by the Eucharist into agape. "Perichoresis" is the Greek word for "moving around," but also the Scholastic term for the explication of the text in John (17.21) in which Christ prays for all believers, "That they all may be one; as thou, Father, art in me, and I in thee, that they also may be one in us." The precise English equivalent of *perichoresis* is "circumincession," which includes the signification of the reciprocal being of all three persons of the Trinity in each other. "Co-inherence," a term favored by Charles Williams, is the one Simeon uses for the same idea in his meditation in "For the Time Being." The abiding tree at the center of the dance is the living Christ.

"Lauds"

The singsong rhythm of "Lauds," derived from the thirteenth-century Spanish Galician *cossante,* which has a repetitive circular form, is a musical equivalent of the tolling of the church bell—"Already the mass-bell goes ding-dong"— that summons people to mass. Following after the penitence of "Compline," "Lauds" is a celebration of worship. The poem opens with a glimpse of nature and the songs of birds:

> Among the leaves the small birds sing;
> The crow of the cock commands awakening:
> *In solitude, for company.*

Auden adapted the chorus of his and Kallman's libretto of *Delia* for "Lauds," making one particularly significant change, replacing the chorus's refrain in *Delia,* "Day breaks for joy and sorrow," with "In solitude, for company." In this stanza and throughout "Lauds," the refrain suggests Auden's personal sense of simultaneous aloneness and union with others in worship at the same time that it represents the church's community of correspondingly unique persons and human beings who are at one in their love of God.

In the second stanza,

> Bright shines the sun on creatures mortal;
> Men of their neighbors become sensible
> *In solitude, for company.*

"Men of their neighbors become sensible," as Mendelson has shown, celebrates the body's senses as a medium of faith and charity. Auden extolled the senses joyfully in 1950 in "Precious Five," the final stanza of which begins by praising the senses and ends by emulating and blessing them:

> Be happy, precious five,
> So long as I'm alive
> Nor try to ask me what
> You should be happy for. . . .
> I could (which you cannot)
> Find reasons fast enough
> To face the sky and roar
> In anger and despair
> At what is going on,
> Demanding that it name
> Whoever is to blame:
> The sky would only wait
> Till all my breath was gone
> And then reiterate
> As if I wasn't there
> That singular command
> I do not understand,
> *Bless what there is for being,*
> Which has to be obeyed, for
> What else am I made for,
> Agreeing or disagreeing?

"Bless what there is for being," of course, was an axiom of Auden's faith, and in both the Swarthmore lecture examining "Prime" and the corresponding article "Nature, History and Poetry" he said that belief in the goodness of existence is an assumption necessary to the writing of poetry. "Precious Five" distinguishes the "I" who protests and must be commanded to believe that goodness from the senses that do so naturally. In "Lauds," the line "Men of their neighbors become sensible," which is repeated in a succeeding stanza, also proposes that it is the senses that first enable human beings to feel love for one another.

The final two stanzas of "Lauds" gather up strands in the earlier poems of "Horae Canonicae":

> God bless the Realm, God bless the People;
> God bless this green world temporal:
> *In solitude, for company.*
>
> The dripping mill-wheel is again turning;
> Among the leaves the small birds sing:
> *In solitude, for company.*

The "Realm" is ruled not by an authority, but by a person, with perhaps the suggestion of the divine right of kings. "People" are not a crowd, but a catholic group of unique individuals. "This green world temporal" includes both nature and history, with their respective cyclical and linear times, and the dripping mill-wheel, which always appealed to Auden, is a construction of the civilized city. The refrain, finally, as it has from the start, celebrates the liturgy, a thing done together, a community of worshippers in church that incorporates the natural and historical beings of each communicant. The whole of "Lauds" is itself a sung Eucharist, one of Auden's most compelling, as the whole of "Horae Canonicae" is a culmination of the expression of Christian faith in his poetry.

Later Years

In the later years of his life Auden's work is character-ized by an increasing acceptance of himself, and a correspon-ding religious sense of gratitude. In his poems, with a few no-table exceptions, he writes more genially of his body, attends lovingly to the domestic circumstances of his daily life, and is disposed to write uncomplicated devotional verse. He becomes increasingly interested in forgiveness, thankfulness, and prayer. The first poem in "Profile," for example, an autobiographical collection of haiku he began in 1965 or 1966, is an ironic prayer:

> He thanks God daily
> that he was born and bred
> a British Pharisee.

The last poem, added in 1973, the year of his death, is reverent:

> He has never seen God,
> but, once or twice, he believes
> he has heard Him.

As the latter haiku suggests, Auden considered prayer an act of listening. In his last major essay, which sums up most of the central articles of his faith, he praises work, carnival, and prayer.

Auden's late phase is anticipated in an earlier work, "In Praise of Limestone," perhaps the most moving poem in his canon. In one of his later collections of poetry, *About the House* (1965), Auden offers thanksgiving for his habitat and celebrates the spiritual as well as physical comfort of individual rooms of his house. "In Praise of Limestone," written in 1948, celebrates his home in nature, the limestone uplands of the Pennines in which he grew up as a boy. The poem's immediate subject is the limestone landscape of Italy, where Auden had just begun to live in the summers, but it looks back as well to the landscape of his youth, the scenery of his personal Eden. In a lecture on Freud in 1971, he said that "In Praise of Limestone" was one of a series of poems dealing with the lead-mining world of his childhood: "The lead-mines, of course, could not come in, because there aren't any in Florence, but the limestone landscape was useful to me as a connecting link between two utterly different cultures, the northern protestant guilt culture I grew up in, and the shame culture of the Mediterranean countries, which I was now experiencing for the first time."

The poem begins descriptively:

> If it form the one landscape that we, the inconstant ones,
>   Are consistently homesick for, this is chiefly
> Because it dissolves in water. Mark these rounded slopes
>   With their surface fragrance of thyme and, beneath,
> A secret system of caves and conduits; hear the springs
>   That spurt out everywhere with a chuckle.

The secret system of caves and conduits and springs anticipates the lines in "Nones" in which Auden talks about the
valves within the human body that close and open, the glands
that secrete, and the vessels that expand and contract to allow
fluids to renew exhausted cells. The outer contours of the
body and landscape in "In Praise of Limestone" are maternal:

> examine this region
>   Of short distances and definite places:
> What could be more like Mother or a fitter background
>   For her son, the flirtatious male who lounges
> Against a rock in the sunlight, never doubting
>   That for all his faults he is loved; whose works are but
> Extensions of his power to charm?

Auden goes on to describe the inhabitants of that landscape,
and how, "accustomed to a stone that responds," to a landscape of human scale—touchable, walkable, nourishing, domestic—they never had to veil their faces in awe of a crater,
or look into the infinite space of a desert, or encounter a
jungle, or be lured by the voices of the granite wastes, purring
clay or gravel, or the ocean that declares, "'There is no love; /
There are only the various envies, all of them sad.'" In a letter
to Elizabeth Mayer, Auden said that the theme of "In Praise
of Limestone" is "that rock creates the only truly human landscape, i.e. when politics, art, etc. remain on a modest un-
grandiose scale. What awful ideas have been suggested to the
human mind by huge plains and gigantic mountains."

His letter, however, describes only one of the themes of
the poem. After his description of "Immoderate soils where
the beauty was not so external, / The light less public and the
meaning of life / Something more than a mad camp," Auden

suddenly addresses his loved one, presumably Kallman, and acknowledges a degree of rightness in the inhuman voices of the other landscapes:

> They were right, my dear, all those voices were right
> And still are; this land is not the sweet home that it looks,
> >   Nor its peace the historical calm of a site
> Where something was settled once and for all.

The limestone landscape is "not quite," he continues, a womb, with "a certain seedy appeal," but "has a worldly duty which in spite of itself / It does not neglect." It "calls into question / All the Great Powers assume; it disturbs our rights." It reproaches the scientist as well as the poet, both the antimythological poet (with allusions to Wallace Stevens) and a poet like himself:

> >   for what
> And how much you know. Not to lose time, not to get
> >   caught,
> >   Not to be left behind, not, please! to resemble
> The beasts who repeat themselves, or a thing like water
> >   Or stone whose conduct can be predicted, these
> Are our Common Prayer, whose greatest comfort is music
> >   Which can be made anywhere, is invisible,
> And does not smell.

But to be free of the repetition and predictability of the human body, to have the comfort of transcendent music, unlocalized and without smell, would be our final wishes only if all we had to look forward to were "death as a fact." "But if," Auden says,

> Sins can be forgiven, if bodies rise from the dead,
> >   These modifications of matter into

Innocent athletes and gesticulating fountains,
    Made solely for pleasure, make a further point:
The blessed will not care what angle they are regarded
    from,
    Having nothing to hide.

"The blessed . . . / Having nothing to hide" anticipates the paradisal ending of "Compline" in "Horae Canonicae," where Auden writes, "That we, too, may come to the picnic / With nothing to hide, join the dance." The final lines of "In Praise of Limestone" are an expression of the hope of love and of faith:

Dear, I know nothing of
Either, but when I try to imagine a faultless love
    Or the life to come, what I hear is the murmur
Of underground streams, what I see is a limestone
    landscape.

The "if"s in "In Praise of Limestone," as well as Auden's admission that he "knows nothing" of either a faultless love or the life to come, are typical of Auden's capacity to believe and to doubt at the same time; and perhaps not unlike the process of *felix culpa*, they paradoxically strengthen, they do not diminish, the Christian promise toward which the poem aspires. "The forgiveness of sins" and "the resurrection of the body" are phrases in the Apostle's Creed, and the undertones of the liturgy of "Common Prayer" at the end of the poem reinforce Auden's quest to translate the Edenic memory of past childhood innocence and maternal love into an adult hope for the future, as the limestone landscape of the Pennines is recreated in the Italian landscape in which Auden wrote the poem. The process of recreation also relates the pleasure given by

the art of limestone statues and fountains, as well as of the
poem itself, to the potential blessedness of the human body,
of which the limestone landscape is an image. And finally, the
process of the religious recreation of the body and landscape
suggests the promise of the resolution of the duality of flesh
and spirit in a love in which there is nothing to hide, in which
eros is fulfilled in agape.

Auden never ceased to struggle with this duality, even in
his later years, and never could be altogether free of the sense
that it required an effort of faith to sustain the belief he was not
simply a passenger in his fleshly motorcar. The poem "You,"
with its complaints about the body and its smell of "being," is
a vivid example of this continuing conflict. For the most part,
however, the poems he composed in his last years testify to his
religious celebration of his being. In "Talking to Myself," a
poem dedicated to Oliver Sacks he wrote in 1971 that is in
counterpoint to the exasperation with his body in "You," he
celebrates his Austrian home and its landscape as well as the
"mortal manor, the carnal territory / alloted to my manage":

> You have preserved Your poise, strange rustic object,
> whom I, made in God's Image but already warped,
> a malapert will-worship, must bow to as Me.

He records his body's instinctive passivity compared to animals with their fangs, talons, hooves, and venom. "Our marriage," he says to his body,

> is a drama, but no stage-play where
> what is not spoken is not thought; in our theatre
> all that I cannot syllable You will pronounce
> in acts whose *raison-d'être* escapes me. Why secrete
> fluid when I dole, or stretch Your lips when I joy?

"For dreams," he says,

> I, quite irrationally, reproach You.
> All I know is that I don't choose them: if I could,
> they would conform to some prosodic discipline,
> mean just what they say. Whatever point nocturnal
> manias make, as a poet I disapprove.

"Thanks to Your otherness," Auden continues, still addressing his body,

> Your jocular concords,
> so unlike my realm of dissonance and anger,
> You can serve me as my emblem for the Cosmos.

Sacks writes in his tribute to Auden that "Wystan felt, in the most literal, tangible, immediate way, that every organ had its place in the body, as every man had his place in the world," and that "Talking to Myself" beautifully expressed his "sense of the body as a home, as a landscape, only conscious on the surface, but going deeper and deeper, into the infinite depths of our world-home, the cosmos."

"Talking to Myself" concludes,

> Time, we both know, will decay You, and already
> I'm scared of our divorce: I've seen some horrid ones.
> Remember: when *Le Bon Dieu* says to You *Leave him!*,
> please, please, for His sake and mine, pay no attention
> to my piteous *Don'ts*, but bugger off quickly.

The religious spirit of these lines, as of the entire poem, is clearly thankful, and one may doubt that Auden himself would have experienced the drama of dying he describes, even if he had not, in fact, had the good fortune to die peacefully in his sleep, his "realm of dissonance and anger" as well as his body at rest.

"Lullaby," written in 1972, constitutes another version of "Talking to Myself." It is a lullaby in which the poet talks to himself as he is going to sleep and treats himself as both an infant and its mother. It begins with domestic details:

> Peace! Peace! Devoid your portrait
> of its vexations and rest.
> Your daily round is done with,
> you've gotten the garbage out,
> and answered some tiresome letters. . . .
> Now you have license to lie,
> Naked, curled like a shrimplet,
> jacent in bed, and enjoy
> its cosy micro-climate:
> *Sing, Big Baby, sing lullay.*

"Cosy," as Sacks points out, with its complementary concepts of belonging, propriety, place, was one of Auden's favorite words for all creatures, animal as well as human, at home in the world and in their bodies.

The second stanza of "A Lullaby" is inimitable Auden:

> The old Greeks got it all wrong:
> Narcissus is an oldie,
> tamed by time, released at last
> from lust for other bodies,
> rational and reconciled,
> For many years you envied
> the hirsute, the he-man type.
> No longer, now you fondle
> your almost feminine flesh
> with mettled satisfaction,
> imagining that you are
> sinless and all-sufficient,

snug in the den of yourself,
Madonna and *Bambino:*
Sing, Big Baby, sing lullay.

In a letter to E. R. Dodds on 18 May 1972, Auden wrote,
"The second stanza of *A Lullaby* is, of course, a bit satiric.
The phantasy of being *'sinless and all-sufficient'* is certainly
not 'rational': I know quite well I am neither." But the satire
is only slight, since Auden seriously as well as playfully imagines a return to the pre-Oedipal innocence of childhood, including the pre-Oedpial union with the mother. Auden had
anticipated the conceit of the combination of mother and
child many years earlier in his discussions of Falstaff's fat-
ness in the essay "The Prince's Dog" in 1959 as well as in
his lecture on *Henry IV, Parts One and Two* and *Henry V* at
the New School in 1946. He said in the essay that a fat
man "looks like a cross between a very young child and a
pregnant mother. . . . The Greeks thought of Narcissus as
a slender youth but I think they were wrong. I see him as a
middle-aged man with a corporation, for, however ashamed
he may be of displaying it in public, in private a man with
a belly loves it dearly; it may be an unprepossessing child
to look at, but he has borne it all by himself." Auden's re-
statement of this theme in "Lullaby" is equally playful and
at the same time has deliberate religious overtones. *"Madonna* and *Bambino; / Sing, Big Baby, sing lullay"* evokes the
description of religion—"Roman Catholic in an easygoing
Mediterranean sort of way"—in the catalogue of his personal Eden.

The third stanza begins with the line "Let your last thinks
all be thanks," which could be an epigraph for the later years

of Auden's life. He thanks his parents (for the strength of his superego), his friends, and the boyhood in which he was

> permitted to meet
> beautiful old contraptions,
> soon to be banished from earth,
> saddle-tank loks, beam-engines
> and over-shot waterwheels.
> Yes, love, you have been lucky:
> *Sing, Big Baby, sing lullay.*

The final stanza prepares for sleep, "oblivion," letting

> the belly-mind take over
> down below the diaphragm,
> the domain of the Mothers,
> They who guard the Sacred Gates,
> without whose wordless warnings
> soon the verbalising I
> becomes a vicious despot,
> lewd, incapable of love,
> disdainful, status-hungry.

The stanza concludes: "*Sleep, Big Baby, sleep your fill.*" The entire poem is at once a fantasy of sleep as a return to Eden and a thankful preparation for the real oblivion of death.

The poetry of Auden's later years also includes devotional poems of great purity, two of which may serve as examples of the reverence as well as inspiration of his faith: the narration to *The Play of Daniel,* a neglected medieval mystery play, which was first brilliantly performed in New York in 1958 as an opera, with music by the New York Pro Musica Antiqua, directed by Noah Greenberg; and the luminous "Ballad of Barnaby," which was written on commission for performance at a girl's school in Connecticut in 1968, with choral accompaniment composed by the students at the school.

The tone of *The Play of Daniel*, at once everyday and liturgical, is immediately set in the opening lines of Auden's narration:

> Welcome, good people, watch and listen
> To a play in praise of the prophet Daniel,
> Beloved of the Lord.

The narration proceeds to describe Nebuchadnezzar's end, the ascent to the throne by his son Belshazzar, "Flushed and foolish, flown with pride," and Belshazzar's feast at which his wives' "shouts grow shameless . . . / In honor of idols of their own devising / Forgetting God from whom all greatness comes." A hand appears and writes on the wall, and the prophet Daniel, famed for wisdom and piety, is summoned to read the writing. He interprets it as a prophecy of Belshazzar's fall, whereupon Belshazzar repents and acknowledges the powerlessness of kings compared to the power of God. As death takes Belshazzar, he declares, "'Let me turn to the Truth, entrust my soul / To the Lord of Light, the Living God!'"

Darius the Great, who "Slays Belshazzar, sits on his throne," raises Daniel to high office, preferring "him over / Presidents and princes," and plans to make him ruler of the realm. In order to trap Daniel, the lords of Darius's kingdom, "Wroth" and "Jealous of this Jew," devise a law stating that all who ask a petition of anyone save Darius must be thrown to the lions. Darius, "thinking no evil," signs and seals the law, allowing the jealous lords to accuse Daniel: "Daniel has dared disobey thee; / Openly he asks for help from his God." Darius is compelled to throw Daniel into the lions' den, but with the aid of the Lord, Daniel is not harmed, and Daniel's accusers, "The princes and presidents who plotted evil / Rue their wrong." They are themselves thrown into the lions' den, and "Ere they reach the bottom / Their bones are broken, their bodies rent, / Torn in pieces by the teeth of the lions."

Daniel is "restored to his state of honor / and dwelt in peace until his days' end." Visions of events to come are revealed to him, including the vision that

> in fullness of time,
> The wise Word that was from the beginning,
> Maker of all things, should be made flesh
> And suffer death to redeem mankind.

The narration ends with "tidings of great joy":

> A baby is born in Bethlehem City
> Who is called Christ, our King and Savior.
> Sing Glory to God and good-will,
> Peace to all peoples! Praise the Lord!

Daniel's prophecy of the Nativity and Incarnation reproduces the medieval mystery drama's portrayal of Old Testament episodes as prefigurations, often elaborate ones, of the revelations of the New Testament; and the cadence and language of the whole of Auden's narration of *The Play of Daniel* are like those of the mystery plays. Unlike "For the Time Being," however, which, as Auden explained to his father, was a modern adaptation of the mystery play, and which showed the meaning of the Cross in everyday twentieth-century life, Auden's narration of the play is a strictly historical rendering of an Old Testament episode, which Auden could treat as a form of worship when he donned the habit of a monk and read it aloud in a series of performances in an Oxford church in 1960.

"The Ballad of Barnaby" is derived from the thirteenth-century *Tombeur de Notre Dame* and is similar in spirit to Auden's narration for *The Play of Daniel,* though it is more jaunty and contemporary in tone and feeling. It begins,

> Listen, good people, and you shall hear
> A story of old that will gladden your ear,
> The Tale of Barnaby, who was, they say,
> The finest tumbler of his day.

The poem continues, with kindly wit,

> His eyes were blue, his figure was trim,
> He liked the girls and the girls liked him;
> For years he lived a life of vice,
> Drinking in taverns and throwing the dice.

One day, as he is traveling between two cities, he sees two ravens "perched on a gallows-tree," who predict that he "'Will one day be as this hanging man'" and that "'when that day comes he will go to Hell.'" Barnaby's "conscience smote him sore; / He repented of all he had done heretofore." He comes to a monastery: "As its bells the Angelus did begin, / He knocked at the door and they let him in."

In the monastery, a place of learning and devotion, "The Abbot could logically define / The place of all creatures in the Scheme Divine" (minus the Thomistic logic, not unlike Auden's own assumption of the unity of truth), the other monks wrote books and Latin sequences, and one of them sang "The praise of Our Lady in the vulgar tongue." After an interlude of choral music, the ballad continues:

Now Barnaby had never learned to read,
Nor *Paternoster* knew nor *Creed*
Watching them all at work and prayer,
Barnaby's heart began to despair.

Down to the crypt at massing-time
He crept like a man intent on crime:
In a niche there above the altar stood
A statue of Our Lady carved in wood.

"Blessed Virgin," he cried, "enthroned on high,
Ignorant as a beast am I:
Tumbling is all I have learnt to do;
Mother-of-God, let me tumble for You."

Straightway he stripped off his jerkin,
And his tumbling acts he did begin;
So eager was he to do Her honor
That he vaulted higher than ever before.

(*Ballet music*)

The French Vault, the Vault of Champagne
The Vault of Metz and the Vault of Lorraine,
He did them all till he sank to the ground,
His body asweat and his head in a swound.

Unmarked by him, Our Lady now
Steps down from Her niche and wipes his brow.
"Thank you, Barnaby," She said and smiled;
"Well have you tumbled for me, my child."

Barnaby continues to "pay Her his devoirs" by tumbling in
front of the statue, and when the Abbot is told and observes
him, he declares, "This man is holy and humble." Following
another interval of ballet music, the ballad continues:

"Lady," cried Barnaby, "I beg of Thee
To intercede with Thy Son for me!",
Gave one more leap, then down he dropped,
And lay dead still, for his heart had stopped.

Then grinning demons, black as coal,
Swarmed out of Hell to seize his soul:
"In vain shall be his pious fuss,
For every tumbler belongs to us."

(*Ballet music*)

But Our Lady and Her angels held them at bay,
With shining swords they drove them away,
And Barnaby's soul they bore aloft,
Singing with voices sweet and soft.

CHORUS: *Gloria in excelsis Deo.*

"The Ballad of Barnaby" is not one of the more ambitious of
Auden's poems, but its relative simplicity beautifully matches
the simple piety of its subject. Barnaby watches the monks "at
work and prayer," and his tumbling for Our Lady is his union
of both. "The Ballad of Barnaby" itself is Auden's own offering of the joining of the two.

Around 1970, Auden wrote an essay entitled "Work, Carnival and Prayer," which was his last major prose statement of
his faith. He advances some new ideas, rehearses many, sometimes with a new emphasis, that he had held for decades, and
presents them all in the widest possible context. Auden begins the essay with his usual prophetic consciousness of the
threat of environmental disaster caused by the plundering,
poisoning, and possible nuclear contamination of the earth,
and he asks what man's duties are to the cosmos as well as the

earth. "Those of us who are Christians or Jews," he says, may
very properly turn for answers to the implications of the story
of Creation in the first two chapters of Genesis, and the exegesis of these chapters underlies most of the essay. He points
out, as he had, at least partly, in several earlier essays, that in
the first chapter we are told "firstly, that the creation of
human beings is only the last in a series of creative acts by
God"; and "secondly, after each of them, the phrase 'And God
saw that it was good' is repeated." "Thirdly," Auden continues, "in blessing human beings, God uses the same phrase
which he used in blessing the animals: 'Be fruitful and multiply'"; and "lastly, it is to be noticed that, in the phrase "Male
and female created He them,' the pronoun is in *the Third
Person Plural*." "That is to say," Auden notes, "though human
beings, unlike minerals and plants and the other animals,
have been made 'in the image of God,' . . . we, like everything
else in the universe, inanimate and animate, are God's creatures." The biblical exegesis Auden then develops is characteristically unparochial and suggests the breadth of his sense
of religious connection to the entire universe. Clive James has
observed that Auden was "a man in whom all cultural history
is present," in "whose prose all the artists of the past are alive
and talking to each other." The community of the universe
and the infinity of the conversations within it were much the
same for him.

Repeating ideas he had previously elaborated in numerous essays, Auden proceeds to discriminate the deities of
Greek culture: first, the polytheistic gods of Greek tragedy,
who are not creators, who are not "'good,'" and whose natures
are indistinguishable from those of men, but who are immortal, invulnerable, and to be feared; and second, the *to Theon*

of Greek philosophy (Platonic Ideas or Aristotle's First Cause) who did not create the universe but is coeternal with it, who is absolutely good and to be loved not feared by men, but who does not love in return. In the cosmology of Plato and Aristotle, "the source of human evil and suffering is not sin, but the misfortune of being souls who are imprisoned in matter, which is by nature inferior and peccable." "Both the gods of polytheism and the god of philosophy," Auden notes, "are alike in that belief in either is not a matter of faith. Worldly success and failure are self-evident facts: logical reasoning leads to inevitable conclusions."

On the other hand, for the biblical God, Auden explains, "no proofs of His existence are water-proof. But if, by faith, we believe in Him and the account of how we were created, certain conclusions follow." The first is that "the basic ground for loving God must be gratitude, not fear"; and the second is that we cannot attribute evil and sin "to the fact that we are not disembodied angels, but creatures of flesh and blood, with the desires, like hunger and sex, which go with that condition." Third, Auden says, "Wittgenstein must be right in saying: 'Ethics does not treat of the world. Ethics must be a condition of the world, like logic.'" That means, Auden explains, that the laws of man's spiritual nature must be like those of his physical nature, which he can by choice or ignorance *defy* but can no more *break* than he can break the law of gravity. Auden then speaks of the great misfortune, because of the Bible's use of the imperative voice, of the Church's choosing the analogy of criminal law—laws *for,* rather than laws *of*—to speak of sin and the punishment of sin, since sin is a violation of the very nature of our being and is its own punishment. In a draft version of this passage, Auden wrote,

"I think the Church to-day should preach more not less about Hell and the possibility of eternal damnation which free-will necessarily implies, but it cannot do so in terms of a criminal court which condemns human souls against their will to eternal torment. If there are any souls in Hell, it is because Hell is where they defiantly insist on being."

Auden says the second chapter of Genesis makes clear that a man is at once an individual member of a species and a person, an "I," who is the creation of God and society and not of a biological process. "Life might be easier for us," Auden continues, "if our awareness of ourselves as individuals and persons could be kept distinct. Unfortunately, they cannot, because man is a history-creating creature who has been able to develop after his biological evolution was complete. . . . It is this duality of our nature that tempts us into Pride, the sin which Christian theologians have always regarded as the Primal Sin, from which all the others issue." Seeking to explain the sin of pride "with as few theological presuppositions as possible," Auden says that his senses can recognize other individuals, but that only an act of faith on his part can enable him to recognize that they enjoy a unique personal existence, as he does. At the same time, though his own personal existence is self-evident to him, it likewise takes an act of faith for him to believe that he is an individual, a member of the human species, "brought into this world by an act of sexual intercourse and exhibiting socially conditioned behavior, to believe, that is to say, that the Self of which I am aware and I are an indissoluble unity. . . . The refusal to make these two acts of faith is what constitutes the sin of pride." Auden's relentless exploration of the duality of the self was a function of his own particular temperament, but as this and other essays in his later years make clear, it was also increasingly a form of religious meditation.

The consideration of the sin of pride leads Auden to a discussion of prayer: "As an antidote to pride," he writes, "man has been endowed with the capacity for prayer, an activity which is not to be confined to prayer in the narrow religious sense of the word. To pray is to pay attention or, shall we say, to 'listen' to someone or something other than oneself. Whenever a man so concentrates his attention—be it on a landscape, or a poem or a geometrical problem or an idol or the True God—that he completely forgets his own ego and desires in listening to what the other has to say to him, he is praying." This definition of prayer has a close affinity to Auden's depiction of vocation, which he usually praises, though his praise is dependent upon the object of the vocation. In "Sext" vocation is turned into an agency of the Crucifixion. Thus, the choice of attention in prayer, Auden notes, "to attend to this and ignore that—is to the inner life what choice of action is to the outer. In both cases a man is responsible for his choice and must accept the consequences. As Ortega y Gasset said: 'Tell me to what you pay attention, and I will tell you who you are.' The primary task of the schoolteacher is to teach children, in a secular context, the technique of prayer." Auden taught in schools and colleges in England and the United States during much of his life, and by all accounts he taught his students that technique. He informed a literature class at the University of Michigan in 1941, for example, that the final exam would require them to write from memory six cantos of Dante's *Divine Comedy*. After incredulous protest

from the students, the number was reduced to five cantos.
They memorized them, and at least one of the students testified that he was forever grateful.

Auden calls "petitionary prayer . . . a special case, and, of
all kinds of prayer, I believe, the least important. Our wishes
and desires—to pass an exam, to marry the person we love, to
sell our house at a good price—are involuntary and therefore
not in themselves prayers, even if it is God whom we ask to attend to them." "They only become prayers," Auden writes, "in
so far as we believe that God knows better than we whether
we should be granted or denied what we ask. A petition does
not become a prayer unless it ends with the words, spoken or
unspoken—'Nevertheless, not as I will, but as Thou wilt.'"
"Perhaps the main value of petitionary prayer," Auden continues, "is that when we consciously phrase our desires, we
often discover that they are really wishes that two-and-two
should make three or five, as when St. Augustine realised that
he was praying: 'Lord, make me chaste, but not yet.'"

Concluding his discussion of prayer, Auden stresses that its
"essential aspect . . . is not what we say, but what we hear." "I
don't think it matters terribly," he writes, "whether one calls
the Voice that speaks to us the voice of the Holy Spirit, as
Christians do, or the Reality Principle, as psychologists do, so
long as we do not confuse it with the voice of the Super-Ego,
for the Super-Ego, being a social creation, can only tell us
something we know already, whereas the voice that speaks to
us in prayer always says something new and unexpected, and
very possibly unwelcome." "The reason why I do not think the
label matters that much," he remarks, "is because I know that
the most convinced atheist scientist has prayed at least once in
his life, when he heard a voice say: 'Thou shalt serve Science.'"

The inclusiveness of Auden's conception of prayer is characteristic of his unusual capaciousness of thought, but it should not be misconstrued, certainly not in his own case, as cavalier. In his tribute to Auden, James Stern recalled an episode when they were together in Germany in 1945, working for the U. S. Air Force Strategic Bombing Service: "One morning on the Starnberger See, where we had to work *en masse* in a vast room and sleep *en masse* in dormitories, I rose very early in order to finish in peace the writing of a long interview of the previous day." "I had hardly settled down at the typewriter," Stern wrote, "when I felt the unmistakable sensation that I was not alone. I glanced up, and there in the furthermost corner, beyond rows of empty desks and chairs, with his back to me but his head turned, sat Wystan—his face a study of anguish fighting with fury. I was already out of the room, I think, before realizing fully that I had disturbed him in prayer."

After his discussion of prayer in "Work, Carnival and Prayer," Auden turns again to Genesis, pointing out two tasks with which God entrusts Adam. First, he is to give proper names to all the animals. "To give someone or something a Proper Name is to acknowledge it as having a real and valuable existence, independent of its use to oneself, in other words, to acknowledge it as a neighbor. . . . As Wittgenstein said: '*I* is not the name of a person, nor *Here* of a place, and *This* is not a name. But they are connected with names. Names are explained by means of them. It is also true that it is characteristic of physics not to use these words.'" Second, Auden points out, "God commanded Adam to till and dress the Garden of Eden . . . to act upon and modify his environment. Man, from the beginning that is to say, was created a worker—work was not imposed upon him as a result of the Fall."

The model offered for all work and, as the Latin word implies, for all culture, Auden continues, is agriculture, which helps to clarify the commands in the first chapter of Genesis to "'replenish the earth and subdue it: and have dominion . . . over every living thing that moveth upon the earth.'" Auden emphasizes that the achievement of dominion depends upon a friendly collaboration between man and Nature, that "only those commands can be fruitful which it is in the true interests of Nature as well as his own to obey." The effects of modern science upon man's relation to nature, Auden says, have been both admirable and pernicious. "On the one hand it has liberated men from a misplaced humility before a false god. The god whose death Nietzsche announced was not the true God, though, undoubtedly, he was the god in whom many people who imagined they were true Christians, believed, namely a Zeus without Zeus's vices." "The great achievement of the sciences," Auden continues, "has been to demythologise the Universe. Precisely because He created it, God cannot be encountered in the Universe—a storm, for example, is a natural phenomenon, not as in polytheism, the wrath of Zeus—just as when I read a poem, I do not encounter the author himself, only the words he has written which it is my job to understand. The universe exists *etsi Deus non daretur* [even if God were not a given]." Such a view, popularized in the writing of Dietrich Bonhoeffer, is germane to much of Auden's work, to "Musée des Beaux Arts," for example, as well as his lecture on *King Lear,* and to his insistence that belief in the Incarnation must be a matter of faith, not reason. Auden stressed at the start of his sermon at Westminster Abbey that by this view of God and the universe he did not mean "a Gnostic religiosity which would have us avert our eyes from the created phenomenal world to gaze at its Creator whom no man hath seen at any time—which is as if a man were to say—O I never listen to Mozart symphonies because it distracts me from thinking about Mozart."

The pernicious effects of science, Auden says, include using our biological evolution from less complex creatures as an excuse for bad behavior. He quotes Karl Kraus: "When a man is treated like a beast, he says, 'After all I'm human.' When he behaves like a beast, he says: 'After all, I'm only human.'" Auden objects as well to the way "scientists speak of 'random' events as if this was a demonstrable scientific fact. It is not. To say an event is 'unpredictable,' at least in our present state of knowledge, is a factual description." "To call an event random," Auden insists, "conceals, without admitting it, a metaphysical presupposition, which lies outside the realm of science altogether, namely the dogma that there cannot be such a thing as Providence or miracles. As a Christian, I believe in both by faith: I don't pretend I can prove them." Goethe, Auden notes, was right in saying that "'we need a categorical imperative in the natural sciences as much as we need one in ethics.'" "We are finding out to our cost," Auden adds, "that we cannot enslave nature without enslaving ourselves. If nobody in the universe is responsible for man, then we must conclude that man is responsible, under and to God, for the Universe." "This means," Auden continues, "that it is our task to discover what everything in the universe from electrons upwards could, to its betterment, become, but cannot become without our help. This means re-introducing into the sciences a new notion of teleology, long a dirty word."

Last, Auden turns to carnival, a subject in which he had become interested as a result of reading Mikhail Bakhtin's

Rabelais and His World in 1968. He notes two characteristics of man that the Bible does not mention, that man is "the only creature who can laugh and the only creature who can play-act, that is to say, pretend to be somebody else." "Laughter," Auden says, "originates in protest but ends in acceptance," and he describes the disarming effects of laughter in much the way he had described the effect of Falstaff on an audience. Men can also play. Animals when they play, play themselves, and human beings similarly remain themselves as game-players, but play-acting is different. "When we play-act," Auden says, "we imitate the words, gestures, and actions of some person other than ourselves, and at the same time . . . remain aware that we are not the person whose role we have assumed. Why on earth should we enjoy doing this? My own conclusion is that the impulse behind play-acting is a longing to escape into a world of pre-lapsarian innocence." This is true also of games, Auden notes, but when we play games such as football or bridge, "our game actions are in themselves innocent, ie, outside the realm of ethical judgement. But when we imitate another human being, we imitate a sinner, and at the same time are not guilty of his sins." We cannot be guilty of them, Auden continues, because our imitative actions are always incomplete. A person does not actually murder anyone if he is playing Macbeth; his actions are mock-actions, his feelings mock-feelings. It is thus "only in play-acting that human beings can approximate the moral innocence of the animals."

"If this is so," Auden writes, "it may help to explain the social and religious function of Carnival, a celebration known equally well to Paganism and to medieval Christianity, but now, at least in industrialised and Protestant cultures, largely

and, in my opinion, disastrously forgotten." Auden then quotes
at length from Goethe's account of the mock sexuality and
mock aggression of a Roman carnival he witnessed in 1788.
To these mockeries, Auden notes, "should be added another
feature typical of most medieval carnivals, mock religious
rites which the Church authorities had the good sense to tol-
erate. They seem to have realized that what holds good for literary parody holds good for all parody, namely, that one can
only successfully parody something one loves and respects."

The world of carnival, a succession of "'happenings'" in
which everybody plays the role of his own choosing, Auden
writes, is "the antithesis of the everyday world of work and action. . . . During Carnival all human beings, irrespective of sex
or age or worldly status, are equal." But Auden adds that it
must be remembered that a carnival lasts only for a week at
the most, and that this week immediately precedes Lent, "the
season dedicated to fasting, repentance, and prayer." In the
worlds of both carnival and prayer, Auden continues, "we are
all equal before Nature as members of the same biological
species: in prayer, we are equal in the eyes of God as unique
persons. The only occasion upon which both forms of equal-
ity are simultaneously asserted is during Mass, at which we
both pray and eat."

Auden cautions, however, that if the spirit of carnival is
prolonged, it must be sustained by stimulants like drugs, it
leads to a rejection of the everyday world, mock actions become real ones, and the fun becomes ugly. He affirms, however, that "carnival has its proper and necessary place. Without it, prayer almost inevitably becomes Pharisaic or Gnostic,
and when men think only of work and ignore both prayer and
carnival, then they lose all humility, all reverence either for

God or the natural universe, all sense of their neighbor, and become the tyrannical exploiters of nature and each other, which is the most obvious characteristic of the societies in which we now live." "Prayer, Work, Laughter," Auden concludes, "we need them all."

AFTERWORD

In one of the many autobiographical haiku he wrote
toward the end of his life, Auden said that

> His thoughts pottered
> from verses to sex to God
> without punctuation.

The progression of thought Auden describes is true to much
of his poetry. It also, unfortunately, can be offensive to some
readers and critics. The lack of punctuation, the conjunction
of his homosexuality and his Christian faith, and perhaps most
of all, the doubts that his intellectual consciousness brought
to bear on all three subjects—verses, sex, and God—can appear to reflect an absence of seriousness and integrity, though
this poem is itself an instance of Auden's integrity and defines
the serious interest, "the interest itself," of his life and work.
Include the humor that embraces it, and the haiku is a tem-

plate of his Christmas letter to Kallman in 1941, "The Temptation of St. Joseph," "In Praise of Limestone," the later "Lullaby," and a host of other poems.

Auden considered his writing of verse a religious calling, he dedicated himself to a rigorous and unyielding daily work schedule throughout his life, and he was from the first extremely ambitious. He told his tutor Neville Coghill at Oxford, for example, at their initial meeting, that he was "going to be a poet." When Coghill politely said, "Well, in—in that case you should find it very useful to have read English," Auden replied after a silence, accurately if precociously, "You don't understand, I am going to be a great poet." He dedicated himself to the writing of poetry in the 1930s and emigrated to the United States to provide the income to keep writing, as well as to escape the class-consciousness and what he called "the suffocating insular coziness" of the English intellectual establishment. And he was unabashedly proud of his mastery of metrics:

> Vain? Not very, except
> about his knowledge of metre,
> and his friends.

But at the same time Auden steadily insisted on the limits of poetry, particularly after reaffirming his faith. The major burden of Caliban's address to the audience in *The Sea and the Mirror* is that art is an illusion of an illusion, holding the mirror up to nature rather than to "the real Word which is our only *raison d'etre*." Auden said that "along with most human activities," art "is, in the profoundest sense, frivolous. For one thing, and one thing only, is serious: loving one's neighbor as one's self." He was highly critical of the pretensions of poets and writers, Romantics particularly, but others as well, including Dante, Milton, and Joyce, who treated poetry itself as a religion, and he especially praised Shakespeare for his humility, for suggesting, "as Theseus does in *A Midsummer Night's Dream*, that 'The best in this kind are but shadows' (V.i.214), that art is rather a bore." He said toward the end of his life that artists fatally delude themselves and shockingly overestimate their importance if they suppose that making works of art can in any way eliminate the evils of this world or alleviate human misery, and he noted that Europe's political and social history "would be what it has been if Dante, Shakespeare, Goethe, Titian, Mozart, Beethoven, *et al.* had never existed." Earlier, in 1951, he wrote that while reading Rilke's letters or the journal of Henry James, "there are times when their tone of hushed reverence becomes insufferable and one would like to give them both a good shaking"; and he remarked that "similarly, the incessant harping on money in the correspondence of Baudelaire or Wagner provokes in the most sympathetic admirer the reaction of a sound bourgeois— 'Why doesn't he go and look for a job?'"

In an essay in 1948 he wrote that the Greeks "confused art with religion" because they were "ignorant of the difference between seriousness and frivolity. . . . In spite of this, they produced great works of art. This was possible because in reality, like all pagans, they were frivolous people who took nothing seriously. Their religion was just a camp." But we, Auden noted, "whether Christians or not, cannot escape our consciousness of what is serious and what is not." He wrote in *The Dyer's Hand* in 1962, "A frivolity which is innocent, because unaware that anything serious exists, can be charming, and a frivolity which, precisely because it is aware of what is serious, refuses to take seriously that which is not serious, can be profound."

These views help explain the change in the style as well as subjects of Auden's poetry after his emigration to the United States. Some critics have seen a decline, if not collapse, of poetic power in the American, as opposed to the English, Auden. This opinion is held especially, though certainly not exclusively, by English critics who cannot forgive either his absence from England during the Blitz (though he tried to enlist in the service in the United States and was rejected), or the indecorum of his move from England to America, proper literary traffic—James, Eliot, for example—having been in the opposite direction. But whatever their perspective, the critics who are disappointed in the later Auden object most to what Seamus Heaney has called "a certain diminution" of the "language's autonomy" and "its wilder shoots" that he exhibited in his poetry in the 1930s, as well as to his practice of significantly revising some poems and throwing out others that represented what he could no longer believe to be "the case." But Auden's restraint of his vast lyric powers and his consequent disciplinary focus upon metrical virtuosity, as well as the revisions of his poems and canon, may also be understood as acts of religious humility, acknowledgments that poetry is not magical or sacred, and that like all things of this world it is a vanity. Auden's doubts about his art are Christian doubts, and the American Auden is emphatically a Christian Auden— which may be yet another, and often unacknowledged, reason for the depreciation of the achievement of his later poetry.

Auden had analogous, and often related, reservations about his homosexuality. In a discussion of "The Sea and the Mirror" in a letter to Christopher Isherwood, he wrote that he expected critics "to jump on the James pastiche" he used to depict Caliban "and think it is unseemly frivolity. Art is like queerness. You may defend it or you may attack it. But people never forgive you if you like it and laugh at it at the same time." Auden tended to see a dialectical relationship between his art and his homosexuality. In a draft of "For the Time Being," Simeon (characterized as a poet) says, "Whenever there is a gift there is a guilty secret, / A thorn in the flesh, both are given together / And the nature of one depends on the other." Auden repeated this Pauline image of "a thorn in the flesh" in his review of Dag Hammerskjöld's *Markings* in 1964, in which he wrote that Hammerskjöld was an example of a man "endowed with many brilliant gifts" who at the same time has "an ego weakened by a 'thorn in the flesh' which convinces him that he can never hope to experience what, for most people, are the two greatest joys earthly life has to offer, either a passionate devotion returned, or a lifelong happy marriage." Two decades earlier, Auden had expressed a similar idea, more hyperbolically but with a different inflection, in a review of Henry James in which he said that "to be a good husband and father is a larger achievement than becoming the greatest artist or scientist on earth," but that being free of marriage and parenthood nonetheless allows the artist to be faithful to his vocation: "Maybe that is why many writers, James among them, have suffered from physical or psychological troubles which made marriage impossible; their disability was in fact, not, as some psychologists assert, the cause of their gift, but its guardian angel."

Auden could not speak of his homosexuality publicly, but in private, with friends, he acknowledged his homosexuality freely and sometimes, as Edmund Wilson remarked, pugnaciously. He had occasional affairs with women and was a friend to a great many people who were not homosexual, and to their families—as Ursula Niebuhr remarked, he always sought the warmth and ballast of family settings—but the story of his personal life is also the story of his homosexual attachments, many of them casual, some intense, and one, his love for Chester Kallman, a focal point of his existence. He believed that "all pleasures are good" if they do not become compulsive, and he wrote to James Stern in 1944, "I may recommend celibacy to the readers of the New York Times, but I do object to being made to practise what I preach."

He made a similar statement about practicing what one preaches in "New Year Letter" in 1940, and in the same year he also wrote, repeating in verse a passage in *The Prolific and the Devourer,* that as a boy grows up he will find that the vulnerabilities and demands of his body will be

> Hostile to his quest for truth;
> Never will his prick belong
> To his world of right and wrong,
> Nor its values comprehend
> Who is foe and who is friend.

Auden's homosexuality may have intensified this Pauline dualism in his consciousness and contributed as well to his lifelong preoccupation with the manifold ways that the relation of body and mind made human beings problematic to themselves. In addition, his expressed views of his homosexuality and its consequences were sometimes skeptical. In 1947, he told Alan Ansen, "I've come to the conclusion that it's wrong to be queer, but that's a long story. Oh, the reasons why are comparatively simple. In the first place, all homosexual acts are acts of envy. In the second, the more you're involved with someone the more trouble arises, and affection shouldn't result in that. It shows something's wrong somewhere." In the same conversation, he also remarked to Ansen that "sexual fidelity is more important in a homosexual relationship than in any other. In other relationships there are a variety of ties. But here, fidelity is the only bond." In a review written in 1969, near the end of his life, he said, "Few, if any, homosexuals can honestly boast that their sex-life has been happy." He also voiced regrets about the loneliness of his homosexual existence. He wrote to Elizabeth Mayer in 1943, "Being 'anders wie die Andern' has its troubles [*Anders als die Andern*, "Different from Others," was the first sympathetic film treatment of homosexuality, made in 1919]. There are days when the knowledge that there will never be a place which I can call home, that there will never be a person with whom I shall be one flesh, seems more than I can bear, and if it wasn't for you, and a few—how few—like you, I don't think I could." In a birthday letter he sent to Ursula Niebuhr in August 1947, he wrote, "I don't think I am over-anxious about the future, though I do quail a bit sometimes before the probability that it will be lonely. When I see you surrounded by family and its problems, I alternate between self-congratulation and bitter envy."

Finally, Auden insisted on the balance of doubt in his religious faith. He repeatedly quoted Pascal's dictum, "To deny, to believe, and to doubt well is to man as the race is to a horse," and he not infrequently talked about religion with "Mediterranean" easiness. He never denied the existence of God, but his belief in God's existence can sometimes sound provisional, and some critics have been inclined to dismiss his faith as more mythological than Christian (though they might consider Ursula Niebuhr's observation that his fascination with the imagery and mythology of Christianity made him more theological, not less). He was not interested in the after-life or eschatological issues and always entertained doubts about the Resurrection. His understanding of Christianity as a Way in which all men and women can participate, rather than as a state, tended to allow fewer boundaries, and there-fore less definition, for a specific faith, and both the latitude and particular "reticence" and humility of his orthodoxy can sometimes trouble believers and nonbelievers alike.

On the other hand, as he himself often pointed out, there cannot be doubt without belief, and Auden's faith was clearly the matrix of his existence. He said in a notebook that "the story of ritual is a hobby of mine," and he was devoted, of course, to the language and performance of the Anglican liturgy, in which he could be at once alone and in a commu-nity of worshippers united in the love of God, each one of an-other, simultaneously expressing their common humanity and their individual uniqueness. Oliver Sacks says that Auden's "religion (like so much else in him) was at once intensely pri-vate and public: he prayed in a solitary and silent mode, but he also liked to lift up his voice in prayer, in a community, in a church, in a chorus of voices; choirs and choruses, for him, were emblems and microcosms of the choragium of nature." The Anglican monk Gregory Dix observes in *The Shape of the Liturgy* that "no liturgy is simply a particular 'way of saying your prayers,' which would be only an instrument for one de-partment of life. Prayer expresses a theology or it is only the outlet of a blind and shallow emotion; and like all prayer a liturgy must do that." "But because it carries prayer on to an

act," Dix continues, "every eucharistic liturgy is and must be
to some extent the expression of a conception of human life
as a whole. It relates the individual worshipper to God and
His law, to redemption, to other men, to material things and
to his own use of them. What else is there in life?" This basically describes the meaning of Auden's faith: his relation to
God and His laws-*of* rather than laws-*for,* as he was fond of repeating; his corresponding relation to other people, his neighbors, as fellow members of a species as well as individual persons; his belief that Christians must enact their faith in the
here and now; his belief that, like all human beings, he could
be forgiven his fallen condition and be redeemed.

Auden believed absolutely, as a matter of faith and not
reason, in "the coming of Christ in the form of a servant who
cannot be recognized by the eye of flesh and blood." At the
same time he saw the Incarnation as an embodiment of the
inseparability of the sacred and profane in all human life, and
as an anti-Manichaean, anti-Gnostic paradigm of the need for
Christians to accept themselves and others as bodily creatures. He believed in the critical importance of the idea of
original sin, including Saint Augustine's view that because
man's will was itself corrupted by the Fall, he is perpetually
subject to temptation and anxiety; and he believed one must
accept the consequent inescapability of human suffering. He
also believed in man's responsibility for his own choices, a belief that underlies his poetry as well as all his criticism. He repeatedly examined the description in Genesis of how God
created man and the universe and saw that it was good and
how God made man responsible for both his fellow creatures
and for the earth itself. He believed in the possibility of ful-
filling eros in agape, as the Law is fulfilled in Mercy. He be-

lieved in providence and miracles, not least the miracle of his own unique existence—Auden's belief in "individualism," in this sense, was profound—and he was continuously refreshed by his apprehension of the wondrousness and hallowedness of ordinary, everyday life. He had a passion for order—"So obsessive a ritualist / a pleasant surprise / makes him cross"—and he believed in "the unity of truth," all truths connected with and reflecting one another, a belief that gives even his most personal poems their unusual scope and resonance, their capacity to relate his experiences to the history and life of the world. And he treasured the possibility of "coziness" for human beings and all other creatures and objects in the universe, all belonging, all in their proper place in their God-given homes.

But perhaps the most compelling characteristic of Auden's thought is the sense of the comic that informs his dialectic of faith and doubt. He wrote that "doubts, unlike denials, should always be humorous," and suspected "that without some undertone of the comic / genuine serious verse cannot be written to-day." Even Auden's most serious doubts, consequently, are voiced with life-forgiving enjoyment, with the undertone of carnival that he insisted must include the mockery of religion as well as of authority and sex. Ursula Niebuhr records that he and her husband Reinhold loved to play ecclesiastical parts in parlor performances and family charades: "Wystan would be an English bishop preaching at a public school. He would blow out his cheeks and intone in a manner both vacuous and impressive to suit the uttered clichés. Reinhold used to enact a frontier American evangelist, and then both of them would portray the particular sins of religion: pride, sloth and self-righteousness."

This kind of fun demonstrates Auden's repeated observation that one parodies what one values, that "one can only blaspheme if one believes." His own capacity for reverent parody and comedy dilates and enriches almost all of his essays and poems, including those explicitly devoted to religious faith. It can be seen throughout his depiction of Joseph in "For the Time Being"—"*Mary may be pure, / But, Joseph, are you sure?*"—a portrait that is richly humorous at the same time that it represents Auden's grief over Chester Kallman's infidelity, as well as his faith in accepting it. The same combination of fun and seriousness animates the refrain of "Shepherd's Carol":

> *O lift your little pinkie*
> *And touch the winter sky*
> *Love is all over the mountains*
> *Where the beautiful go to die.*

When this verse was read at memorial services for Auden in both New York and Oxford, the laughter of the congregations was indistinguishable from their tears. A similar union of the playful and the serious is shown in Auden's description of himself in the stanza in "A Lullaby" that moves from the statement "The old Greeks got it all wrong: / Narcissus was an oldie" to the refrain "*Madonna* and *Bambino* / *Sing, Big Baby, sing lullay*," and that is immediately followed by the line "Let all your last thinks be thanks." The grace of his humor is also shown in the wonderful description of Barnaby in the "The Ballad of Barnaby":

> His eyes were blue, his figure was trim,
> He liked the girls and the girls liked him.

One can imagine the delight of the schoolgirls for whom Auden wrote the ballad when they first heard these lines. A more sophisticated comedy, finally, is revealed in "Horae Canonicae," often gravely ironic: "our victim . . . who knows already . . . that by sundown / We shall have had a good Friday," in "Terce"; sometimes simply amused: "Can poets (can men in television) / Be saved?" in "Compline." Both the irony and the amusement underlie the orchestration of different tones and levels of diction that enables the poem to reflect such a breadth of human experience.

A mixture of the comic and the serious in the treatment of religion also characterizes Auden's prose. He wrote in a notebook, "I can see . . . what leads Tillich to speak of God as 'Ground of Being,' but if I try to pray: 'O Thou Ground, have mercy upon us,' I start to giggle." In "Knight of the Infinite," a review of a biography of Gerard Manley Hopkins, he speaks of how much of a trial Hopkins must have been to the Jesuit Order in which he served, and concludes, "He didn't matter: he had a silly face; he was a martyr to piles; he bored his congregations and was a joke to his students; he fiddled around with Egyptian and with Welsh and with Gregorian music; he wrote a few poems which his best friends couldn't understand and which would never be published; after forty-four years he died. Yes, like Don Quixote." "His poems," Auden continues, "gloss over none of the suffering and defeat, yet when we read them, as when we read Cervantes, the final note is not the groan of a spiritual Tobacco Road, but the cry of gratitude which Hopkins once heard a cricketer give for a good stroke, 'Arrah, sweet myself.'" Finally, the extraordinary balance of Auden's sense of the comic, even when dealing with the gravest of religious subjects, can be seen in his brilliantly poised dismissal of Hilaire Belloc's reported statement that it must be terrible for the Jews, "'poor darlings . . . to be born with the knowledge that you belong to the enemies of the human race . . . because of the Crucifixion.'" "I cannot believe," Auden replies, "that Mr Belloc is an altogether stupid man. Nevertheless, his statement is on a par with Adam's 'The woman beguiled me and I did eat.' He can hardly be unaware that the Crucifixion was actually performed by the Romans, or, to make it contemporary, by the French (the English said, 'Oh dear!' and consented; the Americans said, 'How undemocratic!' and sent photographers) for the frivolous reason that Jesus was a political nuisance." "The Jews who demanded it," Auden continues, "did so for the serious reason that, in their opinion, Jesus was guilty of blasphemy, i.e., of falsely claiming to be the Messiah. Every Christian is, of course, both Pilate and Caiaphas."

The unusual combination of objectivity, sympathy, and enjoyment in these examples of Auden's comic understanding of the flesh and the spirit suggests that the most remarkable feature of his remarkable intelligence may have been its generosity. Auden was hardly a saint, but by all accounts from the great range of people of whose friendship he was proud, he was a kind man, whose compassion was "rooted," as he said compassion must be, in a delight in existence and in thankfulness, "in wonder, awe, and reverence for the beauty and strangeness of creation." Geoffrey Grigson wrote in a tribute to Auden that "not all of his poems are kind, but most of them are," and that "inseparable from his kindliness" was his Christian faith. I think that's right. Auden was a great poet and critic, but he should also be remembered, and would have wished to be remembered, as a man who sought to lead a Christian life.

NOTES

ABBREVIATIONS

Auden's Works

EA   *The English Auden: Poems, Essays and Dramatic Writings 1927–1939,* ed. Edward Mendelson (London: Faber and Faber, 1977).

Prose I   *The Complete Works of W. H. Auden: Prose,* vol. I: 1926–1938, ed. Edward Mendelson (Princeton: Princeton University Press, 1996).

Prose II   *The Complete Works of W. H. Auden: Prose,* vol. II: 1939–1948, ed. Edward Mendelson (Princeton: Princeton University Press, 2002).

CP   *Collected Poems,* ed. Edward Mendelson, 2d ed. (New York: Random House, 1991).

DM   *The Double Man* (New York: Random House, 1941).

TSTM   *The Sea and the Mirror,* ed. Arthur Kirsch (Princeton: Princeton University Press, 2003).

LS   *Lectures on Shakespeare,* reconstructed and edited by Arthur Kirsch (Princeton: Princeton University Press, 2000).

EF   *The Enchafèd Flood: Or The Romantic Iconography of the Sea* (New York: Random House, 1950).

DH   *The Dyer's Hand* (New York: Random House, 1962).

RT   Notes on Religion and Theology, 1966–67 holograph notebook in the Henry W. and Albert A. Berg Collection, New York Public Library.

SW   *Secondary Worlds* (London: Faber and Faber, 1967).

ACW   *A Certain World: A Commonplace Book* (New York: Viking, 1970).

FA   *Forewords and Afterwords,* selected by Edward Mendelson (New York: Random House, 1973).

WCP   "Work, Carnival, and Prayer," TS, with Auden's handwritten corrections, in the Berg Collection. Extracts from the essay were published posthumously in *Episcopalian* 138. 3–5 (Mar.–May, 1974).

Other Sources

Later Auden   Edward Mendelson, *Later Auden* (New York: Farrar, Straus and Giroux, 1999).

Early Auden   Edward Mendelson, *Early Auden* (New York: Viking, 1981).

Fuller   John Fuller, *W. H. Auden: A Commentary* (Princeton: Princeton University Press, 1998).

Carpenter   Humphrey Carpenter, *W. H. Auden: A Biography* (London: Allen and Unwin, 1981).

Tribute   *W. H. Auden: A Tribute,* ed. Stephen Spender (London: George Weidenfeld and Nicolson, 1974).

INTRODUCTION

Page

xi   "prudery": Review of Reinhold Niebuhr, in *Prose* II, 131.

xi   Auden praised Saint Augustine: *Prose* II, 228.

xii   "there is the Faith": In "Religion and the Intellectuals," *Partisan Review* 17 (February 1950), 121.

xii   "Art is not metaphysics": *Prose* II, 87.

xii   "An argument followed": Robert Medley, *Tribute*, 40.

xiii   "Kicking a little stone": *CP*, 110.

xiii   "lost his faith": *FA*, 517.

xiii   random events: Auden wrote in "Talking to Myself," "Unpredict-
       ably, decades ago, You arrived / among that unending cascade of
       creatures spewed / from Nature's maw. A random event, says Sci-
       ence. / Random my bottom! A true miracle, say I, / for who is not
       certain that he was meant to be?"

xiii   luminous essays on Christianity: "Lecture Notes," *The Common-
       weal* (6 November-4 December 1942), in *Prose II*, 161–72.

xiv   introduction to Anne Fremantle's: *FA*, 69–70.

xiv   became active in: See Ursula Niebuhr, *Tribute*, 116; and Mendel-
       son, *Later Auden*, 280.

xiv   comprehensive and eloquent essay: WCP (Berg Collection).

xiv   in the same essay: "Religion and the Intellectuals," 121–22.

xiv   "are written by and for believers": *FA*, 518.

xiv   "the right thinking": *Prose* II, 250.

xv   "our faith . . . well balanced": "New Year Letter," line 962. All refer-
       ences to "New Year Letter" line numbers and notes are to the text
       in *DM*.

xv   "In a civilized society": *Prose* II, 103.

xv   "Human law rests": *Prose* II, 425.

xv   "basic stimulus": *FA*, 51.

xv   skepticism . . . must be founded upon reverence: *SW*, 126.

xv   "To doubt for the sake of doubting": *FA*, 51.

xv   Ursula Niebuhr . . . wrote: *Tribute*, 106.

xvi   characteristically open-minded answer: Letter to Ursula Niebuhr,
       13 May 1941 (Library of Congress), cited with slight variation in
       Tribute, 106.

xvi   In a sermon . . . at Westminster Abbey: Typescript MS, with Au-
       den's handwritten corrections (Westminster Abbey Archives). Auden
       repeated the "shaggy-dog" remark in *SW*, 136 and *ACW*, 173; and
       he repeated the anecdote about Niel Bohr in *SW*, 143.

xviii "The Church as a whole": RT (Berg Collection). Auden's notes on
       religion and theology were incorporated in *SW*; in *ACW*; in the
       typescript MS of Auden's sermon at Westminster Abbey in 1966;
       and in the typescript MS of WCP (Berg Collection).

xviii   "Friday's Child": Unless otherwise noted, the texts of Auden's
        poetry are those of *CP*.

xviii   "A sinless life": Letter to Clement Greenberg, 16 December 1944
        (Clement Greenberg Papers, Archives of American Art).

xviii   "of all the Christian Churches": *FA*, 71.

xix   "overemphasis on one aspect of the truth": *FA*, 183.

xix   Dietrich Bonhoeffer's declarations: *FA*, 192; latter statement also
        quoted in *ACW*, 175.

xix   "All the same, Clem": Letter to Clement Greenberg (Archives of
        American Art).

xx   "has to make his public confession": *Prose* II, 250.

xx   "You can no more pick": *Prose* II, 223.

xxi   letter to Monroe Spears: 19 March 1962 (Berg Collection).

xxi   "In this world": *ACW*, 175.

CHAPTER ONE. EARLY YEARS

1   "the Christian doctrine": In *Modern Canterbury Pilgrims and Why
        They Chose the Episcopal Church*, ed. James A. Pike (New York:
        Morehouse-Gorham, 1956), 32–33. Auden described the essay as
        "rather shy-making" in a letter to Ursula Niebuhr (14 July 1955),
        cited in *Remembering Reinhold Niebuhr*, ed. Ursula M. Niebuhr
        (San Francisco: Harper San Francisco, 1991), 288.

2   "In my opinion sermons": RT (Berg Collection). Two decades ear-
        lier, he said in a "worried" letter to Ursula Niebuhr (14 February
        1946), regarding one of Reinhold Niebuhr's sermons: "Looking
        round at my fellow congregation, I felt the effect was to make them
        smug." He added that "Kierkegaard as usual put his finger on the
        sore spot when he said that the task of the preacher is to preach
        Christ the contemporary offense to Christians." (*Remembering Rein-
        hold Niebuhr*, 284–85.)

2   Services on Sunday: *Prose* II, 414.

2   cherished such childhood memories: Auden also stressed the im-
        portance of childhood religious excitement in a review in which he
        deplored the conviction of sin that was bred in Kierkegaard at an
        early age by his father. "What Christian parents in their senses,"
        Auden wrote, "ever spoke to a child about God in Christ accepting

sinners. If they are intelligent, they will see that a child's first encounter with the religious life should be aesthetic, not reflective, with exciting rituals, not with sermons. . . . it is wicked to talk to a child about sin or guilt. One can only speak of the difference between a good little boy and a bad little boy. Good little boys do what is expected of them when put on the potty and do not pull their sisters' hair. Good little boys get candy; bad little boys get none" (*FA*, 190–91).

2   Two other "saving" influences: *Modern Canterbury Pilgrims*, 37.

3   Ursula Niebuhr noted: *Remembering Reinhold Niebuhr*, 280.

3   his outraged response: *ACW*, 225–26. In the same passage on the reform of the liturgy, Auden also objected to the proposed deletion of the Prayer of Humble Access and the General Confession, the "interminable and boring" extensions of the Prayer for the Church Militant, and the omission of the *Filioque* clause from the Creed. In a letter to Ursula Niebuhr from Austria on 30 August 1972, after Reinhold Niebuhr died, Auden wrote, "I have, naturally, thought about writing something for Reinhold, but can't see my way. To write a successful elegy, one has to combine the personal theme with an impersonal. R. was a theologian, and the only theological bee in my bonnet is Liturgical Reform, which wasn't his province. Did I tell you that, since my own parish church went mad, I am reduced to going to a Russian Orthodox Church?" (*Remembering Reinhold Niebuhr*, 294).

3   "his ice-cold imagination": David Ayerst, cited in Carpenter, 47.

3   Other friends . . . wrote: See, e.g. Orlan Fox and David Luke, *Tribute*, 173, 205.

4   "At sometime or other": *Prose* I, 13.

4   "belief in the existence": *ACW*, 283.

4   Christopher Isherwood remarked in 1937: Reprinted in *Tribute*, 74, 76.

4   Stephen Spender . . . said: *World Within World* (London: Faber and Faber, 1951), 54–55; cited in Carpenter, 77.

5   "As you know": letter to Stephen Spender, ?late April-early May 1940 (Berg Collection), edited by Nicholas Jenkins, in "*The Map of All My Youth*," Auden Studies 1 (Oxford: Clarendon Press, 1990), 72–73. Auden defined the terms he uses, which were derived from

Carl Jung, in "For the Time Being" ("Annunciation," Part One): "Intuition: As a dwarf in the dark of / His belly I rest"; "Feeling: A nymph, I inhabit / The heart in his breast"; "Sensation: A giant, at the gates of / His body I stand"; "Thought: His dreaming brain is / My fairyland."

5   "because I half suspected": *Prose* II, 44.

5   Robert Medley said: *Tribute,* 42.

5   his brother John said: *Tribute,* 29.

5   "each of us": *Prose* II, 70.

5   "always being out alone": *Prose* II, 109.

6   "Aloneness is man's real condition": "New Year Letter," line 1542. Line numbers and notes to "New Year Letter" refer to *DM*; the text of the poem is that of *CP.*

6   "In every man there is a loneliness": RT (Berg Collection).

6   "in the liturgical and sacramental life": *FA,* 448.

6   "At thirteen. . . . accurately, of anything": *Modern Canterbury Pilgrims,* 33–36. Later in his life, Auden cited 1920 as the beginning of his period of ecclesiastical "*Schwärmerei*" and 1922 as the date that he discovered he had lost interest in his faith (*FA,* 517).

7   "Every Christian has to make": *FA,* 518.

8   "the Catholic emphasizes": *Prose* II, 134.

8   "it is personal experience": *FA,* 55.

8   wrote in a notebook: RT (Berg Collection).

9   "The various 'kerygmas' . . . endless series of cycles": *Modern Canterbury Pilgrims,* 38.

9   *The Orators: An English Study:* Text in *EA.*

10   "Narcissus": In W. H. Auden, *Juvenilia,* ed. Katherine Bucknell (Princeton: Princeton University Press, 1994).

10   letter to William McAlwee: Cited in Fuller, 61.

10   "liberation from the superego": Cited in Fuller, 60.

10   "Freud if you like": Cited in Fuller, 153.

11   the feast of agape: See Dom Gregory Dix, *The Shape of the Liturgy* (Westminster: Dacre Press, 1945), 82–102.

12   "we are all members": "Two Sides to a Thorny Problem," *New York Times,* 1 March 1953, section 2.

12   "The drunk is unlovely": *DH,* 197.

12   "One fine summer night in June 1933": *FA,* 69–70.

14   review praising Violet Clifton's biography: *Prose* I, 43

14   "O Love the interest itself": Text in *EA*.

14   Isherwood remarked in 1937: *Tribute*, 74.

15   Hannah Arendt wrote: *Tribute*, 182.

16   "happiness consists in": "The Things Which Are Caesar's," *Theology* 53 (November 1950), 417.

16   "for the gift of being alive": *Prose* II, 238.

16   "All freedom implies necessity": *Prose* II, 70.

16   Edward Mendelson observes: *Early Auden*, 237.

17   Isherwood reported: *Tribute*, 79.

17   "What right have I to swear": *CP*, 271.

20   "There may or may not be": *Prose* II, 433.

20   as he put it to Ursula Niebuhr: *Tribute*, 108.

21   Weil's statement: *FA*, 52.

21   "To-day, we find Good Friday": RT (Berg Collection).

21   "despite appearances to the contrary": *FA*, 47; *Prose II*, 429.

21   a letter to Clement Greenberg: 16 December 1944 (Archives of American Art).

21   letter to Monroe Spears: 19 March 1962 (Berg Collection).

21   "novelty and shock of the Nazis,": *Modern Canterbury Pilgrims*, 40.

22   a number of "quite ordinary . . . Germans": Cited in Mendelson, *Later Auden*, 89; Carpenter, 282.

22   "all the churches were closed": *Modern Canterbury Pilgrims*, 41.

23   "an Anglican layman": *Modern Canterbury Pilgrims*, 41. In addition to *The Descent of the Dove* (London: Longmans Green, 1939), Auden may also have been prompted to his conversion by works of C. S. Lewis. In "A Thanksgiving" (1973), Auden wrote, "Wild *Kierkegaard, Williams* and *Lewis* / guided me back to belief."

23   "forced to know in person": *Modern Canterbury Pilgrims*, 41.

24   "Because it is in you, a Jew": From text published in *Later Auden*, 182–83.

25   As Mendelson has remarked: *Later Auden*, 47.

25   Humphrey Carpenter has suggested: Carpenter, 300n.

26   referred to in a letter as his "pensées": Letter to A. E. Dodds, 28 August 1939, cited by Mendelson, *Prose* II, 409.

26   "In using the terms Father and Son": *Prose* II, 430, 431.

27   "Body and Soul (Not-Me and Me)": *EA*, 297–98.

27   "Our bodies cannot love": *CP*, 713.

28   "was able to relate the universal": *Prose* II, 79.

28   "it does seem to me": Letter to Brother Rigney, 4 August 1956 (Berg Collection).

28   "all the striving": *Prose* II, 411.

29   note to "New Year Letter": Note to line 451.

29   "Only in rites": *CP*, 896.

29   Robert Medley spoke: *Tribute*, 40.

29   "mentally precocious": *Prose* I, 55.

29   "total lack of interest in": *FA*, 508.

29   "humiliating performance": *TSTM*, 78 n 6.

29   "one of those persons": *FA*, 374.

30   "The way he dresses": *CP*, 774.

30   "It is unfortunate": Reprinted in *DH*, 131.

30   "the Greek word which St. Paul": *ACW*, 226.

30   "that the Self of which I am aware": WCP (Berg Collection).

31   "the false philosophy": *Prose* II, 424–26.

31   "if we cannot resolve": *Prose* II, 168.

31   "the animals, whose evolution is finished": *Prose* II, 426–27.

32   "all experience is dualistic": *Prose* II, 168.

32   "the dualism inaugurated by Luther": *Poets of the English Language*, ed. W. H. Auden and Norman Holmes Pearson, 5 vols. (New York; Viking, 1950), 1, xxx.

33   "Man is neither pure spirit": *Prose* II, 307–08.

33   "binocular vision": *Prose* II, 56.

33   "the gift of double focus": Lines 828–32, 559–60, 819–22.

33   "The Asiatic cry of pain": Lines 269–70, 273–76.

34   "Gnostics in the brothels": Lines 1310–11.

34   "false and repellant": Letter to Mr. Kenneth Heuer, 17 October 1962. Heuer, of Macmillan publishers, had asked Auden to write an introduction to *Voyage to Arcturus*. Auden responded that "the Gnostic theology upon which it is based is so false and repellant, that in justice to both the author and to Macmillan, I am not the man to write an introduction."

34   "the source of many ideas": Note to line 1600.

34   pointed out by Edward Mendelson: *Later Auden*, 115.

35   "O Unicorn": Lines 1651–57, 1682–84.

35   quotation from Augustine's: Saint Augustine, *The Confessions*, trans.
      William Watts (London: William Heinemann, 1912), X. xxix.

36   "Even Augustine": *Prose* II, 88.

37   as Williams wrote: *Descent of the Dove*, 165.

37   the first time, as Mendelson points out: *Later Auden*, 146.

CHAPTER TWO. FOR THE TIME BEING

40   Augustine mentions: *Confessions*, III. iv.

40   John Fuller observes: Fuller, 346.

41   letter explaining the work to his father: Letter to George Augustus
      Auden (transcribed by him), 13 October 1942 (Berg Collection),
      cited in part by Mendelson, *Later Auden*, 186.

41   in a manuscript note: "[Religion]" (Berg Collection). Edward Men-
      delson notes in conversation that the manuscript "must have been
      written as a commentary to be broadcast (or possibly printed) in as-
      sociation with the Austrian television broadcast of "Inzwischen," a
      musical setting by someone named Paul Kont of parts of "For the
      Time Being," on Austrian television, 5 January 1967."

44   "Joseph is me": Cited in Fuller, 349.

44   what he called "l'affaire C": Letter to Alan Ansen, 27 August 1947
      (Berg Collection).

44   "What does it say": Cited by John Bridgen, *W. H. Auden Society
      Newsletter*, No. 3 (April 1989).

44   "Behind this ingenious": *ACW*, 87; "dogmas to which Wystan": *Trib-
      ute*, 28. John Auden mistakenly wrote "honorary Arian."

45   "the rites of public worship": *ACW*, 175.

45   criticized Kierkegaard: *Modern Canterbury Pilgrims*, 42.

45   "to long for the transcendent": Quoted in *FA*, 192.

45   "Sexuality is only truly": Cited in Bridgen, *Auden Society News-
      letter*, No. 3.

46   as Fuller remarks: Fuller, 349.

47   He wrote his father: Letter to George Auden, 13 October 1942.

48   "occurred precisely": *Prose* II, 133.

48   Buber wrote: *I and Thou*, trans. Ronald Gregor Smith (Edinburgh:
      T & T Clark, 1937), 14–15, 33.

50 "a naturalistic religion": "Religion and the Intellectuals," *Partisan Review* 17, 126.

50 "it's as well at times": *CP*, 567.

50 "It is impossible": *FA*, 51.

50 "abhorred in the Heav'ns": *CP*, 811.

50 "when we use words": *SW*, 127.

50 "I cannot accept": *ACW*, 425.

52 "Instead of the artist": *Prose* II, 117.

52 "what we know of Herod": Letter to George Auden, 13 October 1942 (Berg Collection).

56 aphorism from Franz Kafka: Cited in *The Viking Book of Aphorisms*, ed. W. H. Auden and Louis Kronenberger (New York: Viking, 1962), 92. See also *LS*, 242.

56 "The Light may shine": Letter to Theodore Spencer, 29 April 1943 (Harvard University Archives).

57 derived from Augustine's *Confessions*: VII.x.

57 *"Wenn der Rabbi trennt"*: *ACW*, 249.

57 "is really about the Christian conception": Letter to Ursula Niebuhr, 2 June 1944, *Remembering Reinhold Niebuhr*, 283.

57 "As a writer": *Prose* II, 163.

58 "is my Ars Poetica": Letter to Theodore Spencer, ?24 March 1944 (Harvard University Archives).

58 "There's something a little irritating": *LS*, 319.

58 "Now I want / Spirits": All references to Shakespeare are to the text of *The Complete Works of Shakespeare*, ed. George Lyman Kittredge (Boston: Ginn and Co., 1936). Auden's marked copy of this edition is in the library of Texas Tech University in Lubbock, Texas.

59 "been reading St Augustine": 16 January 1942 (Berg Collection).

59 "As a biological organism": *DH*, 130. First published in "Balaam and the Ass" in *Thought* (Summer 1954).

60 an extraordinarily detailed chart: See Mendelson's transcription of the chart in the Swarthmore College Library, *Later Auden*, 240; reprinted in *TSTM*, 16.

61 "the world of fact we love": All references to *The Sea and the Mirror* are to the text in *TSTM*.

61 the scriptural peril of . . . "the lion's mouth": See Ps. 22.13, 21; 2 Tim. 4.17; and Rev. 13.2.

61   "described to Isherwood": Letter to Christopher Isherwood, April
      1944 (Huntington Library).

62   "more the contemptuous pardon": *DH*, 129.

62   "can give people": *LS*, 306–07.

63   "mutuality of love begets love": MS draft of *TSTM* in the Poetry and
      Rare Books Collection of the Library of the State University of New
      York at Buffalo. Another MS draft, containing material Auden
      transposed from "For the Time Being" to *TSTM*, is in the Berg Col-
      lection of the New York Public Library.

63   Auden told Isherwood: Letter to Isherwood, April 1944 (Hunting-
      ton Library).

63   "I was both the youngest": *ACW*, 5.

64   "those who think of the good life": *Prose* II, 431.

64   "the child, and the child-in-the-adult": *FA*, 389.

65   The passage describes Alice: Quoted at the end of the lecture on
      As You Like It, in *LS*, 151.

66   a speech he considered a masterpiece: Immediately after complet-
      ing *The Sea and the Mirror*, Auden wrote to Elizabeth Mayer, 21
      March 1944 (Berg Collection), "I think the Tempest stuff is the best
      I've done so far"; and to Christopher Isherwood, April 1944 (Hunt-
      ington Library), "I think it is one of the few pieces of mine which
      are 'important.'"

67   "Caliban does disturb me": Letter to Theodore Spencer ?24 March
      1944 (Harvard University Archives).

68   Auden said that James: *Prose* II, 243.

71   "give" and "get": See, e.g., *LS*, 264; "The Things Which Are Cae-
      sar's," *Theology* 53, 412.

CHAPTER THREE. AUDEN'S CRITICISM

73   "A poem must be": *DH*, xii.

73   "criticism is live conversation": Alan Ansen's notes on Auden's lec-
      tures on Shakespeare at the New School (Berg Collection); see
      LS, x.

74   wrote Stephen Spender: Cited in Carpenter, 404.

74   William Empson: *New Statesman* 65 (19 April 1963), 592, 594–95.

74   review of Cochrane's book: *Prose* II, 229–31.

76   "As an agnostic": Dodds, quoted by Auden, *FA,* 41.

76   "As an Episcopalian": *FA,* 41.

77   "One may like or dislike Christianity": "The Fall of Rome," in *"In Solitude, for Company": W. H. Auden After 1940,* Auden Studies 3 (Oxford: Clarendon Press, 1995), 130.

77   "many evils, like slavery": *DH,* 461.

77   "A society which really was": *Prose* II, 348.

78   "by the degree of diversity": *Prose* II, 359.

78   "The assumption of the *Iliad*": *Prose* II, 365–66.

79   "As in Homer, we find ourselves": *Prose* II, 367–68.

79   essay on *Moby-Dick*: *Prose* II, 258.

79   In "The Globe": *DH,* 174–76.

81   "typical of the human condition": *DH,* 99.

81   "No notion of our Western culture": *ACW,* 228–30.

82   "at the root of the romantic": *Prose* II, 138.

82   "diseases of the Christian imagination": *Prose* II, 371.

83   "our present life now repossessed by the Spirit": De Rougemont, quoted in *Prose* II, 139.

83   "For Eros," Auden says: *Prose* II, 139. Auden later found support for his reservations about de Rougemont's vagueness in defining Eros in Martin D'Arcy's *The Mind and Heart of Love* (London: Faber and Faber, 1946).

83   Kierkegaard's statement: Quoted in lecture on *Romeo and Juliet,* in *LS,* 51.

84   Auden . . . disparaged Joyce: *Prose* II, 118.

84   "Like everything which": *ACW,* 248.

84   "What is so puzzling": *FA,* 67–68.

85   "He sees Beatrice": *FA,* 68–69.

86   what Shakespeare believed: *LS,* 312.

87   Eliot's statement in . . . in *After Strange Gods*: Cited in *Later Auden,* 150n. Mendelson quotes Auden's letter to Eliot, as well as his review in *The Griffin* (March 1953) criticizing Eliot's plays, in the same note.

87   unlike Eliot's: Auden did fall under Eliot's spell in his interpretation of the characters of Hamlet and Othello. Like Eliot, he deplored Hamlet's self-absorption, and he ignored Hamlet's growth and emergence from grief in act V, including his explicit recognition

of "special providence in the fall of a sparrow," with its echo of Matthew; see *LS*, 159–65. Auden also had little interest in Othello's suffering, subscribing to Eliot's judgment that in his final speech Othello is basically cheering himself up; see "The Dyer's Hand," *Listener* 53, 1372 (16 June 1955), 1065.

87   "might meet and have dinner with": *LS*, 220.

88   "its presentation of 'worldliness . . . it catches us all'": *LS*, 240, 238, 241–42.

90   "At a performance": *DH*, 183.

90   "Prince Hal. Yes": *LS*, 108, 110.

90   "Why do people get fat?": *LS*, 111.

91   essay on the *Henry IV* plays: *DH*, 197–98, 203–04, 206.

92   Empson: *New Statesman* 65, 592, 594.

92   "I don't care whether": *LS*, 375.

93   "a young schoolgirl": *LS*, 203; *DH*, 268.

93   "just for the hell of it": *LS*, 197–98.

93   Dostoevski's *Notes from Underground*: Quoted in *LS*, 206–07.

93   "a parabolic figure": *DH*, 270, 266.

94   "a world in which": *DH*, 235.

94   "Whenever a society . . . their annihilation": *LS*, 84–85.

95   "Modern anti-Semitism": *Prose* II, 172.

95   "hard cases make bad law": *LS*, 83–84, 81.

96   "the voice of God": *DH*, 125.

96   "the real counterpointing": *LS*, 224–25.

96   lecture on *Troilus and Cressida*: *LS*, 170.

97   "The quality common": *LS*, 220.

97   "This is a profoundly": *LS*, 229.

97   essay on Christianity and art: *DH*, 458.

98   He . . . treated Kafka: *DH*, 159–60. Auden relates a Kafkaesque experience of his own during World War II: "I had spent a long and tiring day in the Pentagon. My errand done, I hurried down long corridors eager to get home, and came to a turnstile with a guard standing beside it. 'Where are you going?' said the guard. 'I'm trying to get out,' I replied. 'You are out,' he said. For the moment I felt I was K" (*DH*, 160).

98   "In the detective story": *DH*, 151, 158. Auden notes that Raymond Chandler, who "has written that he intends to take the body out of

the vicarage garden and give the murder back to those who are good at it," is actually "interested in writing not detective stories, but serious studies of a criminal milieu, the Great Wrong Place, and his powerful but extremely depressing books should be read and judged, not as escape literature, but as works of art."

98   "the real theme of *Pickwick*": *DH*, 408–09.

99   "who possesses authority . . . sane and the mad": *EF,* 93–97.

100   "Don Quixote," Auden argues: *EF,* 103, 101–02.

100   "To have faith in something . . . of their merit.": *Prose* II, 381–82.

101   relation to Sancho Panza: *DH,* 138, 137.

102   "however many further adventures": *Prose* II, 383–84.

103   "an elaborate synecdoche": *EF,* 62, 65.

103   "Kierkegaard's definition . . . greatest in literature": *EF,* 136–37.

104   "*being* what others are not": *EF,* 139–40.

104   "enact every ritual": *EF,* 141–43.

105   a "wicked book": Letter to Nathaniel Hawthorne, ?17 November 1851, *The Writings of Herman Melville,* vol. 14: *Correspondence* (Evanston and Chicago: Northwestern University Press and The Newberry Library, 1993), 212. Melville's full statement was, "I have written a wicked book, and feel spotless as the lamb."

105   Hawthorne wrote: "Journal," November 1856, quoted in *Writings of Melville,* vol. 15: *Journals* (Evanston and Chicago, 1989), 628.

107   luminous quotation: Auden adapts Melville's celebration of his "infinite fraternity of feeling" with Hawthorne in his exultant letter of ?17 November 1851: "I feel that the Godhead is broken up like the bread at the Supper, and that we are the pieces."

CHAPTER FOUR. "HORAE CANONICAE"

109   He told Golo Mann: *Tribute,* 99.

110   "Barthian exaggeration": "Religion and the Intellectuals," *Partisan Review* 17, 123.

110   Tillich's statement: *DM,* 132. I am indebted to Mendelson's penetrating discussion of Tillich, *Later Auden,* 148–53, and *passim.*

110   "The relation of faith": *Prose* II, 381.

110   He especially valued Niebuhr: *Prose* II, 133.

111   manuscript notes for the television broadcast: "[Religion]" (Berg Collection).

112 "As we were all in Adam": RT (Berg Collection). See also *ACW*, 169.

114 As Dom Gregory Dix explains: *The Shape of the Liturgy*, 332.

114 exfoliates into a representation: Auden constructed elaborate conceptual scaffoldings for the sequence in his manuscripts. For a comprehensive discussion of the genesis of the whole of "Horae Canonicae," as well as of each poem in the sequence, see Mendelson, *Later Auden*, 332–59.

114 lecture at Swarthmore College in March 1950: All quotations from the lecture refer to a typed MS transcript in the Swarthmore College Library.

115 "everything that is is holy": *Prose* II, 426.

115 "so long as we have bodies": Foreword to Daniel Hoffman, *An Armada of Thirty Whales* (New Haven: Yale University Press, 1954).

116 "a double act": "The Things Which Are Caesar's," *Theology* 53, 411–12.

117 in his sermon at Westminster Abbey: Westminster Abbey Archives.

117 "I believe . . . because He is": *Prose* II, 196–97.

118 "the experience of waking up": All quotations from the lecture refer to the typed transcript in the Swarthmore College library.

124 St. Barbara became the patron saint: *Later Auden*, 348.

125 "by a love of something other": *SW*, 120.

126 "When the New Testament speaks": *FA*, 43.

127 "When we speak of being born": *FA*, 54.

130 "vanish, *agape* takes their place": *Prose* II, 318.

131 "The Creatures" in 1936: Text in *EA*.

133 Arcadian "knows that his expulsion": *DH*, 410.

134 "while neither Eden nor New Jerusalem": *DH*, 410.

135 "that we are not alone": *FA*, 471.

138 as Mendelson has shown: *Later Auden*, 358–59.

CHAPTER FIVE. LATER YEARS

142 "The lead-mines": Cited in Fuller, 406.

143 The secret system of caves: As both Mendelson and Fuller point out, Auden drew a number of details and phrases in "In Praise of Limestone" from Anthony Collett, *The Changing Face of England* (London: Nisbet, [1926]).

143 "that rock creates": Letter to Elizabeth Mayer, 8 May 1948 (Berg Collection).

147 "Wystan felt": Oliver Sacks, *Tribute,* 190.

148 "Cosy": Sacks discusses Auden's use of this word in *Tribute,* 189.

149 letter to E. R. Dodds: Quoted in Fuller, 551.

149 "looks like a cross between": *DH,* 196.

150 *The Play of Daniel*: Text in W. H. Auden and Chester Kallman, *Libretti and other Dramatic Writings by W. H. Auden 1939–1973,* ed. Edward Mendelson (Princeton: Princeton University Press, 1993), 401–07.

156 "Those of us who are": All quotations from WCP are from the type-script MS (Berg Collection).

156 Clive James has observed: *At the Pillars of Hercules* (London: Faber and Faber, 1979), 37, 23.

157 In a draft version of this passage: RT (Berg Collection).

160 at least one of the students: Donald Pearce, who records the epi-sode in "Fortunate Fall: W. H. Auden at Michigan," in *W. H. Auden: The Far Interior,* ed. Alan Bold (London: Vision Press, and Totow: Barnes and Noble Books, 1985), 153–54. Pearce writes that Auden originally assigned *seven* cantos. Auden himself, in a letter to Ursula Niebuhr (19 December 1941), wrote that he had asked the class to memorize six cantos but said he would reduce the amount if he couldn't "do the assignment" on a train trip from Chicago to Los Angeles (*Remembering Reinhold Niebuhr,* 282).

161 "One morning on the Starnberger See": James Stern, *Tribute,* 127.

AFTERWORD

167 "His thoughts pottered": *CP,* 797.

168 told his tutor Neville Coghill: Recounted by Geoffrey Grigson, *Tribute,* 16.

168 "the suffocating insular coziness": *FA,* 382. This a rare instance of Auden's use of the word "cozy" in a pejorative sense.

168 "Vain? Not very": In "Profile," *CP,* 775.

168 "along with most human activities": *Prose* II, 302.

169 "as Theseus does": *LS,* 319.

169 "would be what it has been": *SW,* 141.

169 "there are times when": *Partisan Review* 18 (Nov.–Dec. 1951), 704.

169 In an essay in 1948: *Prose* II, 345.

169 "A frivolity which is innocent": *DH,* 429.

170 what Seamus Heaney has called: Seamus Heaney, *The Government of the Tongue* (London: Faber and Faber, 1988), 126. Alan Jacobs cites and discusses this quotation, as well as negative judgments of Auden's later career by Philip Larkin and Randall Jarrell, among others, in his study of Auden's later career, *What Became of Wystan* (Fayetteville: University of Arkansas Press, 1998).

171 "to jump on the James pastiche": Letter to Isherwood, 5 April 1944 (Huntington Library).

171 "Whenever there is a gift": Draft of "For the Time Being" (Berg Collection).

171 "an ego weakened": *FA,* 442. Auden also discusses the idea of "the thorn in the flesh" in a review of Louise Bogan, *Prose* II, 155.

171 "to be a good husband": *Prose* II, 244. In a discussion in 1942 of Kafka's troubled relation with his father, Auden wrote similarly that "the true significance of a neurosis is teleological . . . a neurosis is a guardian angel; to become ill is to take vows" (*Prose* II, 112–13). Auden suggests a comparable attitude in *The Orators* at the end of "Letter to a Wound."

171 as Edmund Wilson remarked: *The Fifties,* ed. Leon Edel (London: Macmillan, 1986), 291–92.

172 as Ursula Niebuhr remarked: *Remembering Reinhold Niebuhr,* 280.

172 "all pleasures are good": *ACW,* 304.

172 "I may recommend celibacy": Letter to James Stern, 31 December 1944 (Berg Collection).

172 "Hostile to his quest": "Shorts," *CP,* 297, a variant of his endnote to "New Year Letter," line 51.

172 "I've come to the conclusion": Alan Ansen, *The Table Talk of W. H. Auden,* ed. Nicholas Jenkins (Princeton: Ontario Review Press, 1990), 80–81.

173 "Few, if any, homosexuals": *FA,* 451.

173 He wrote to Elizabeth Mayer: 20 February 1943 (Berg Collection).

173 birthday letter . . . to Ursula Niebuhr: *Tribute,* 118.

174 "the story of ritual": RT (Berg Collection).

174 Oliver Sacks says: *Tribute,* 190.

174   Gregory Dix observes: *The Shape of the Liturgy*, xviii.

175   "the coming of Christ": *DH*, 457.

176   "So obsessive a ritualist": "Profile," *CP*, 775.

176   "Doubts, unlike denials": *ACW*, 35.

176   "that without some undertone": *CP*, 857.

176   Ursula Niebuhr records: *Tribute*, 110.

177   "one can only blaspheme": *FA*, 472.

177   "Shepherd's Carol": Text in *As I Walked Out One Evening*, ed. Edward Mendelson (New York, Vintage: 1995). Auden originally wrote the carol for "For the Time Being" but did not include it in the published poem. It was set to music by Benjamin Britten and broadcast by the BBC in 1944.

177   memorial services: See Orlon Fox, David Luke, and Oliver Sacks, *Tribute*, 176, 194, 217.

178   "I can see . . . what leads Tillich": RT (Berg Collection).

178   "He didn't matter": *Prose* II, 220.

179   brilliantly poised dismissal of Hilaire Belloc's: *Prose* II, 363.

179   "rooted . . . in wonder, awe, and reverence": *FA*, 393.

179   Geoffrey Grigson wrote: *Tribute*, 16.

INDEX